M000266352

Fairy Homes & Gardens

BARBARA PURCHIA AND
E. ASHLEY ROONEY

INTRODUCTION BY DAVID D. J. RAU

Schiffer
Publishing Ltd

4880 Lower Valley Road • Atglen, PA 19310

Other Schiffer Books on Related Subjects:

Fairies, Mermaids, and Other Mystical Creatures: Artist Trading Cards
978-0-7643-2803-9, $29.95

The Twilight Realm: A Tarot of Faery
978-0-7643-3393-4, $34.99

Spiritual Gardens: A Guide to Meditating in Nature
978-0-7643-3731-4, $29.99

Copyright © 2014 by Barbara Purchia and E. Ashley Rooney.

Library of Congress Control Number: 2014941277

All rights reserved. No part of this work may be reproduced or used in any form
or by any means—graphic, electronic, or mechanical, including photocopying
or information storage and retrieval systems—without written permission from
the publisher.

The scanning, uploading, and distribution of this book or any part thereof via
the Internet or via any other means without the permission of the publisher
is illegal and punishable by law. Please purchase only authorized editions
and do not participate in or encourage the electronic piracy of copyrighted
materials.
"Schiffer," "Schiffer Publishing, Ltd. & Design," and the "Design of pen and
inkwell" are registered trademarks of Schiffer Publishing, Ltd.

Designed by RoS
Type set in Affair/Korinna

ISBN: 978-0-7643-4698-9
Printed in China

Published by Schiffer Publishing, Ltd.
4880 Lower Valley Road
Atglen, PA 19310
Phone: (610) 593-1777; Fax: (610) 593-2002
E-mail: Info@schifferbooks.com

For our complete selection of fine books on this and related subjects, please visit our
website at www.schifferbooks.com. You may also write for a free catalog.

This book may be purchased from the publisher. Please try your bookstore first.

We are always looking for people to write books on new and related subjects. If you
have an idea for a book, please contact us at proposals@schifferbooks.com.

Schiffer Publishing's titles are available at special discounts for bulk purchases for sales
promotions or premiums. Special editions, including personalized covers, corporate
imprints, and excerpts can be created in large quantities for special needs. For
more information, contact the publisher.

*Author's Note: For consistency, we have used
the modern spelling of "fairy" instead of "faerie."*

Contents

Rob Heard's daughter and her friend love to play with his Bough Houses. They call them "Fairy Houses" and help test each new house as it appears. They are "like a treehouse, but a dreaming skywards citadel, a sculpture that you explore, a fairytale-esque journeyland to delight the mind's eye." *Courtesy of Elli Ellis.*

4

F*O*R*E*W*O*R*D

Do You Believe in Fairies?

People will tell you that the days of witches and black cats, signs and omens are long gone; those things are only to be found in old wives' tales or stories to frighten children. Those stories, though, are what keep us fascinated on hot summer nights when the thunder rolls and lightning sparks glimpses of what lies in the darkness. Many of these tales are part of our heritage. They are ones we all know — that we have grown up with.

Many supernatural creatures dot our world, particularly when we are children: the fairy godmothers who act as mentors, the trolls of Scandinavia, the Seven Dwarfs, Tinker Belle in *Peter Pan*, the leprechauns of the Irish, and the many other generally invisible elves, pixies, and mermaids who have populated our fairy tales, myths, and legends. They are generally grouped under the umbrella term "fairy." Although we laugh about the tooth fairy and the fairy godmother, many people report sightings of creatures similar to fairies throughout the world.

FAIRY WORLD

Despite all our modern technology, fairies can still inspire gentle dreaming and elaborate worlds. Young children and people with "Second Sight" are said to be able to see the fairies, though they are invisible to all others. Fairies are generally quite small, sometimes with gossamer wings, and usually female. They are perceived to glide along rather than walk. Their preferred color is green.

This fairy has on her favorite pink dress to welcome us into her home and garden, which was designed by Sheryl Lozier.
Courtesy of Whitbeck Photography, San Diego, California.

Some say Fairyland lies in the woods. Others say it is underground, in hills and green mounds of rock or earth, or even underwater. It reveals itself bright and glittering or behind a mist-like curtain. Fairyland time is different than ours, and their lives are quite different.

Previous generations thought that mushrooms appeared where "fairies" had danced the night before. These fairy rings can spell danger for the human. The wild enchantment of the fairy music often draws humans towards the ring, which can lead to an enchanted captivity in Fairyland. If you want to look at fairy rings quite strictly, toadstools consume nitrogen when growing. They tend to spread their spores outward where there is a new supply of nitrogen for spores to grow on…but it is much more fun to look at them as signs of fairies.

Humans who enter Fairyland may pass hundreds of years there, thinking it is only one night. If they are in Fairyland, humans should not eat or drink nor take anything that is not freely given. Those who break these rules may find their world changed forever.

Fairyland is said to be like our world, but much more beautiful. Their palaces are bedecked with gold and silver; residents and guests consume immense banquets of the richest, most delicious food with bejeweled tableware. They dance and listen to music. Fairies are said to be fine gold and silversmiths and excellent metalworkers. They own cattle and have dogs. They grow plants and vegetables and collect fruits for living. They can speak the language of animals.

Fairies like cheerful, generous humans. They like food and wine to be left for them and expect to find a clean and orderly house with no curious eyes watching them. The only way that humans can tell whether a fairy has visited is by the mysterious disappearance of their goods. Fairies often borrow from humans, which accounts for all those things that go missing.

Fairies should be treated with great respect because they can bestow good or bad luck. They help the poor, find lost children, and, if you are good to them, they can bring you good fortune and prosperity. Sometimes, they do small, one-time tasks or they can take on hard work, such as performing chores. When fairies help you, you should leave out a nightly bowl of cream or milk. Fairies do not like to be watched or have people brag about their kindnesses. Their privacy must be respected.

Is this a fairy hovering in the hollow of the tree? *Courtesy of Barbara Purchia.*

FAIRY HOMES AND GARDENS

Today, thanks to the creative spirit of artists, designers, grandparents, and children, fairy homes and gardens have become widespread. Botanical gardens and museums hold participatory exhibits; popular magazines describe how to make fairy log houses or twig chairs for miniature gardens. Garden shops sell miniature plants and fairy furniture and occasionally present "how to make your own fairy garden" seminars. Many are involved in this latest gardening trend. Perhaps it is because fairies reward those who respect the environment with good fortune, joy, and happiness.

When I first considered writing this book, I asked my grandchildren and their friends to come over one hot July day to build fairy houses, and so four children, ages 7-10, spent a happy morning collecting items to decorate their houses, making mud for the houses, collaborating, and cooperating.

My granddaughter later said, "Libby and I found a shady spot to start building a fairy house with pine cone and bark walls. First, we thought about the rooms in a fairy house: the kitchen, bedroom, and living room. We started with the kitchen. We made a mushroom and acorn top sink and used rocks for benches and the table. We thought about the rock benches and decided to cover them with moss. We added a petal tablecloth and placed berries on the table. Then we took a watermelon seed and added mud for chocolate because I think all fairies love chocolate. Next, we made the bedroom. We laid down moss for the mattress and then we put a petal for the pillow and another for the yellow-red blanket. We live in Massachusetts, and fairies probably get cold in the wintertime."

Jay O'Rourke, fairy house designer, instructs, "Start with a broken pot, which is not as easy as it sounds. My first had a crack from top to bottom. Once tapped with a hammer, it broke the sides nicely, but took out much of the bottom of the pot as well. After lining it with a moss mat and saucer, I create the landscape. Secure stacked pots with bamboo stakes and cut below the planting level. Continue to add soil and pack spaces between the pots with sheet moss to prevent a landslide. Different kinds of moss, both natural and preserved, add a variety of colors. Use polished stone or broken pottery for stepping stones. Bonsai soil and smaller polished stones add texture and interest. Plants that stay small are ideal for your fairy garden, but sooner or later, you may have to replace them. Try using club moss, baby's tears, herbs, and succulents for less maintenance."
Courtesy of Kristina Miner.

Libby and Chrissy had a wonderful time working out the details of their house, as did the two boys. It wasn't just the ability to play in the mud, but, rather, the creation that had them so excited.

One friend and her grandchildren believe that if they build a fairy home and leave it, they might attract a fairy into their domain. She and her grandsons, six-year-old Carson and four-year-old Everett, collect crab shells, seaweed, and driftwood for their house. They then decide what their house will look like. The project takes imagination, decision-making, and building skills — something that all children have and love to use (think of the popularity of Legos®).

One of the designers featured in this book, Tatiana Katara, points out that "making fairy houses is about more than just gluing little pieces of bark together or stacking stones into the semblance of a tiny natural home. It's about tuning in and listening to nature. It's about being open to whatever you might see or feel or think about while walking and looking for materials.

"It doesn't matter where you live. Nature is everywhere, even in the cities. If there is a waterfront area, you could find driftwood or shells or smooth round rocks. You may find sand for landscaping or to make mortar with. In the woods, you might find pine needles, dried leaves, bark, moss, snail shells, rocks, and lichen.

"In the city, nature is fighting every day to maintain her presence. You'll see weeds sprouting up between cracks in the sidewalk, and you might find chipped pieces of cement or branches or leaves. If you go to a hobby store, you will find things like feathers and potpourri, and glass marbles and rocks. Look around."

Many grandparents design fairy houses with their grandchildren. Lynne Yansen and Carson Miller, one of her grandsons, pose in front of their fairy house.

TATIANA KATARA

Fairy houses are made from your imagination — and with bark, flowers, rocks, shells, pods, nuts, feathers, beads, buttons, bows, etc. In the following pages, 30 designers portray their fairy worlds in a variety of settings using both natural and contemporary mediums. Many transform the natural world into enchanting art that draws upon our childhood feelings and dreams and recreates a sense of the fantastic. Others draw upon different mediums to express their vision. The fairy homes that result provide a basis upon which to build a story or alter a familiar tale out of recognition. Readers can use this book to admire the creativity of these designers or to build a fairy house or garden themselves. The fairy houses here are built in the woodlands, near the water, and in the meadow. They are built for special events and to tell stories and because, yes, we do believe in fairies!

Fairy house designer Tatiana Katara points out that what you can make from natural materials is almost as limitless as your imagination, especially if you make it in miniature. Natural materials, such as the ones displayed here in her basket, often break down more quickly than manufactured items, so if your fairy house is outside during a harsh winter it may not last.

OH GIVE ME A HOME

When morning comes I spread my wings and flutter through the day;
I bounce on buttercups and pounce on peas in the garden as I play.
I sip the dew drops and dine on seeds, whilst the sun sails duly west;
And when the fireflies twinkle-twinkle, I know it's time to rest.

I pile up leaves beside the creek, while feeling slightly wary,
For the barking dogs and swooshing bats can make the nighttime scary.
Perhaps I should camp high in a tree, or atop the high church steeple,
Or down a dinky dank rabbit hole, away from all the people.

If only I had a home, a haven from the storms.
With a tiny doors and windows, a stone hearth to keep me warm.
Filled with twiggy chairs and tiny books beside a mossy bed,
And a tree bark table stacked with yum where friends will all be fed.

Oh, I'd plant a garden about this little space called home,
With twisting paths and dappled seats beneath the leafy dome.
Protected by a pinecone fence and a gate of twisted vine,
All would be welcome for a visit, but alas, the place is mine.

A dwelling just for faerie folk is what the world is needing.
And this keen book is just the key, so please friend keep on reading.

~ Penned by N. Anon Emous,
a wee one in search of shelter

I·N·T·R·O·D·U·C·T·I·O·N

Making Make-Believe:

A Fairy Architect's Obsession Confession

by David D. J. Rau

One day, not so long ago, I noticed a pile of logs with rotten centers next to a row of neatly stacked firewood beside this grand old house on my way to work. Full disclosure, I love gnarled and twisted wood, especially when I'm in fairy-house-making mode. By the third or so pass, I was obsessed, but it was not the kind of pile you could just help yourself to, it was too near the house, too close to the barking dog. I slowed my red pickup truck and memorized the address. Back at my computer, I Googled the address and eventually found a phone number. I did not want to lose my nerve so I just dialed and prayed to get the answering machine. Ring, ring, ring. The machine picked up.

"Hello," I began. "You don't know me, and I know this is going to sound crazy, but I make fairy houses and I was driving past your house and saw some rotten logs and wondered if you would consider letting me stop by one day and …." on and on I babbled. I did not really expect a call back, and one did not come for over a week, but when it did, the person was genuinely thrilled about my interest in their unburnable wood. In fact, they knew all about my work at the local museum with fairy houses and said that I was more than welcome to the wood.

13

Needless to say, I was like a kid in a candy store loading the muddy and bug-ridden logs, really the size of stumps, into my truck as if I was raiding a Mayan tomb. Back home, I took a hose to the logs, the rushing water sending loads of natural debris and creepy crawly things out of the other end. Once dry, the smooth wooden centers were gorgeous and cave-like and perfect for what would become my fairy house project for the summer. In the end, the logs were transformed into three fairy-scaled caverns, complete with prehistoric-looking wall carvings burned into the wood, shelf fungus balconies, and mossy interiors.

Although I only started creating houses for fairies as an adult (approaching mid-life as long as I live to be 100) a few years ago, it does not seem too far removed from the elaborate sand castles I made each summer as a child on the beach at Peach Lake in the middle of Michigan. Forming walls of sand and decorating the ramparts with pebbles, twigs, and seaweed, to see how tall a tower of sand could stand until a passing motor boat sent the dreaded waves to shore to melt the fragile walls away.

Even today, it's easy to get lured into the miniature world of make believe, where we can build the dwellings of our dreams on sandy islands surrounded by moats and linked to the mainland by tree bark bridges. Instead of spending hundreds of dollars at a home improvement, Big Box-type store, we can raid the tidal pools and sandy pathways for all the materials needed.

Unlike doll-houses, where objects are made to look like tiny versions of the real thing, fairy houses incorporate another level of imagination, transforming rocks and moss into makeshift furniture. It's hard for me to take a walk around the block without returning home with pockets of acorn caps and tiny pinecones. I now know where to harvest last year's dried out bamboo stalks after the spring thaw and cannot pass up the bits of fuzzy moss that blow out of the trees after a windy storm. I must admit to ravaging the walls of the garden cart at work because the peeling wood had just the right patina and would be great for a fairy house wall or roof.

While gathering my items, I have no idea exactly what the bits and pieces of nature will become. Acorn caps start off looking like bowls and hats, but also work great as hanging planters, teapots, and doorknobs. There is also the beach, where the shells, smooth rocks, and sea glass are just the things for lining pathways through fairy gardens and making tiny furniture. I collect sticks for their interesting shapes that inspire curvy fairy stairways and twisting fairy ladders. I also forage for fairy material at tag sales and flea markets. I've used thimbles as vases, fishing flies as flowers, buttons as plates, and even bamboo beads as balustrades for driftwood balconies. Whether the material is found in the forest or at the local corner store, the fairy magic is in the imagination and how these elements are transformed into useful miniature objects for the wee ones.

My advice to the novice fairy architect is this: start by thinking small. See an old stamp as a work of art to be hung on the fairy's wall. Imagine a colorful leaf as a snuggly blanket. Find a dried seedpod and transform it into a magical boat. Almost anything can be something else with a little imagination and careful manipulation. Be like Alice and drink the bottle labeled "Drink Me" and shrink down to the size of a fairy and imagine the spaces you would like to inhabit. How would you spend your day and create the objects necessary? Sure you have wings, but after a long day you might want the assistance of a tiny ladder, a twisty staircase, or even a rope to help you get from one level to the next.

Believe it or not, making fairy houses did start out as my day job. As the Director of Education & Outreach at the Florence Griswold Museum, the Home of American Impressionism, in Old Lyme, Connecticut, I suggested that we build a fairy village on the grounds of the museum as a way to attract new audiences and to celebrate the eleven acres of riverfront gardens and grounds. The idea was that the fairies would be the muses that brought inspiration to the artists who traveled from New York City to the country village of Old Lyme to paint the landscape each summer season. I built a wee fairy dwelling for the fairy "N," the muse to Canadian artist Arthur Heming, who came from the North. It was in an abandoned vegetable crate at the back door and filled with both found and natural materials that made a perfect home for this rough-and-ready fairy. That first October, over 10,000 visitors passed through the museum.

Just last year, the museum mounted another village, this time dedicated to the fairies that inspire the landscape painters by representing all the wonders of nature — from flowers to rivers and all that's in between. This time I built a wee fairy cavern out of those old logs mentioned earlier for the wee fairy Tym-Brrrr, a fairy of dead wood and fallen trees. The museum's second fairy village attracted over 13,000 visitors despite Hurricane Sandy and an early winter storm. Day after day, the fairy village and the incredible creations enchanted visitors of all ages. And so it continues.

In closing, the message throughout this book is to search for the unseen, to marvel in the miniature, and to dream about the yet-to-be imagined enchanted fairy homes to come. Let this be the beginning of your adventure. Consider making a fairy home and provide a safe place for those seeking shelter in the nooks and crannies of your garden, create that home-sweet-home for a fairy that just might live real close by. Anything is possible when you start making make-believe.

David D. J. Rau is the Director of Education & Outreach at the Florence Griswold Museum in Old Lyme, and most recently the coordinator of the Museum's outdoor October events: Wee Faerie Village (2009), Scarecrows at the Museum (2010), Of Feathers and Faerie Tales: Enchanted Birdhouses (2011), Wee Faerie Village in the Land of Picture Making (2012), and Wee Faerie Village in the Land of Oz (2013). He also participates in the events as an artist, honing his skills by building fairy houses, sculpting scarecrows, and decorating birdhouses.

Sally J. Smith of Greenspirit Arts created her Autumn Flame cottage by stitching sugar maple leaves together with needle and cotton thread to form this free-standing house in situ. *Courtesy of Sally J. Smith/Greenspirit Arts.*

Fairies in the Gardens and Meadows

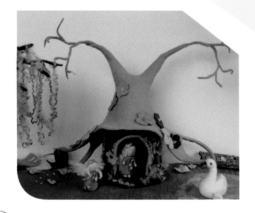

Despite all our modern technology, fairies still inspire gentle dreaming and elaborate worlds. Believers in fairies say they are usually quite small, sometimes with gossamer wings, and usually female. They are perceived to glide along rather than walk. Often you can see fairies flitting through the gardens.

Beth Witsik constructed a Butterfly House from a decorative iron birdcage and festooned it with artificial flowers. She used wood, artificial flowers, fabric, sticks, wire, crystals, berries, acorns, baskets, polymer clay, and knickknacks in designing and building furnishings and accessories. The house gets its name from the numerous butterflies that flit around the roof, which looks as if it were plucked from an English garden. Inside the house, her garden-themed dining area has a checkered silk tablecloth and two flower petal stools. The table is set with silver dollar placemats, an acorn full of sugared fruit, flower petal candlesticks, and a loaf of French bread. Above the table, a ceiling fan made from flower petals keeps a steady breeze blowing.

Carol Betsinger created this whimsical fairy house covered with moss and lichen. Its shape was determined by two different sections of a hollowed-out tree trunk that lost its bark long ago. A crushed stone path leads under the arbor constructed from twisted corkscrew willow branches to an oak bark front door that opens and closes. An unusual fungus protrudes from the roof above the front door. She used leaf skeletons to pane the windows. In the back of the house, at the peak of the roof, a triangular opening leads to a tree fungus balcony. In the light of the full moon, you may be lucky enough to catch a glimpse of fairies dancing there. The steps of the spiral staircase are made of 1/2" peach branch slices. The banister is a twisted branch of the corkscrew willow. Fairies are lured to climb this staircase to frolic on the swing that is suspended from the higher balcony overhead.

19

For a unique take on a fairy bubble house, Roxie Zwicker cut open a grapevine ball and mounted it to two small tree branch stumps. Wired purple berries curl around the house alongside soft reindeer moss. Inside the house is a bed covered in green ivy fabric; a green leaf serves as the headboard. Golden beads hang over the doorway.

Paula Malta tells us that fairy Rose rescued an abandoned vintage makeup case and transformed it into an illuminated two-story treasure with a rooftop terrace. The bird's nest hides the light source. The first floor, with a natural sea glass and tile floor, contains Rose's bedroom with a vintage pincushion and abalone headboard and a vintage crocheted doily for her blanket and a shell lamp, which actually lights up! A vintage button and wood thread spool table and two mini porcelain teacup seats are in the other corner. Hanging from the ceiling is a shabby chic chandelier made from crystal and glass beads and semi-precious stones. Upstairs is her luxurious bath with a seashell and vintage button floor. Accessories include a pink hand towel, sponge, and a tiny shell soap dish.

Fairies tend to be mischievous and love to play practical jokes. Simon Sinkinson knows that when tiny things mysteriously arrive, the fairies are out to play — but in this case, it looks like it is a rogue snail!

Jennie Stockslager uses the basilica design of this gazebo-like lantern to invoke the vision of a hidden spiritual retreat. Certainly, you can see the beginnings of a fairy mushroom ring. Previous generations thought that mushrooms appeared where "fairies" had danced the night before. The wild enchantment of the fairy music can lead humans towards the ring, which can lead to an enchanted captivity in Fairyland. If you really want to examine a fairy ring, you should run around it exactly nine times when the moon is full and in the direction that the sun travels. This way you can hear the fairies dancing underground.

Dani Mendenhall of Dragonfly Hollow designed Harvest Time at the Farm in a ceramic container. She used a miniature scarecrow, vegetables, and plants. The pot makes a charming ornament for the front door.
Courtesy of Kellen G. Peterson.

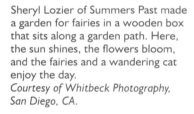

Sheryl Lozier of Summers Past made a garden for fairies in a wooden box that sits along a garden path. Here, the sun shines, the flowers bloom, and the fairies and a wandering cat enjoy the day.
Courtesy of Whitbeck Photography, San Diego, CA.

Paula Malta turned a decorative (re-purposed) metal container on its side and filled it with tiny garden treasures in her Tuscan Garden. A wire rocking chair with a vintage fabric button and a satin ribbon pillow await a guest. The gold metal and wire table is accessorized with wood pots filled with dried baby's breath, tiny shells, a tray with mini buns, a metal Eiffel Tower charm, garden tools, and a *Better Homes and Gardens* magazine. A shell and pearlized paint wood pot birdbath and three-crystal beads plant stake for a sparkle welcome any feathered friends. They can also enjoy a hanging wood birdhouse with a painted red heart. Finally, no garden would be complete without a kitty cat, and note how the birds have built a nest on top with two eggs.
Courtesy of Elisa F. Harvey.

In her Thimble Cottage fairy garden, Dani Mendenhall of Dragonfly Hollow placed a stone cottage with a weathered picket fence and meandering stone paths amidst what appears to be overgrown shrubbery (trailing rosemary) in a moss-filled frame. A mailbox and heart-shaped stepping stones lead us to the front door. Plants include pink and white hypoestes, Scottish moss, trailing rosemary, blue hair grass, and speedwell.
Courtesy of Kellen G. Peterson.

Sally J. Smith of Greenspirit Arts perched her Garden Stone cottage upon a moss-covered boulder in a rock garden. Beavers upstream peeled the willow twigs used as roof rafters, and their teeth marks can be seen on the visible ends. A simple, slender weeping willow twig was shaped and twisted to form a Celtic-styled window. The stone path bridges the gap between the boulders to the garden behind the cottage.
Courtesy of Sally J. Smith/Greenspirit Arts.

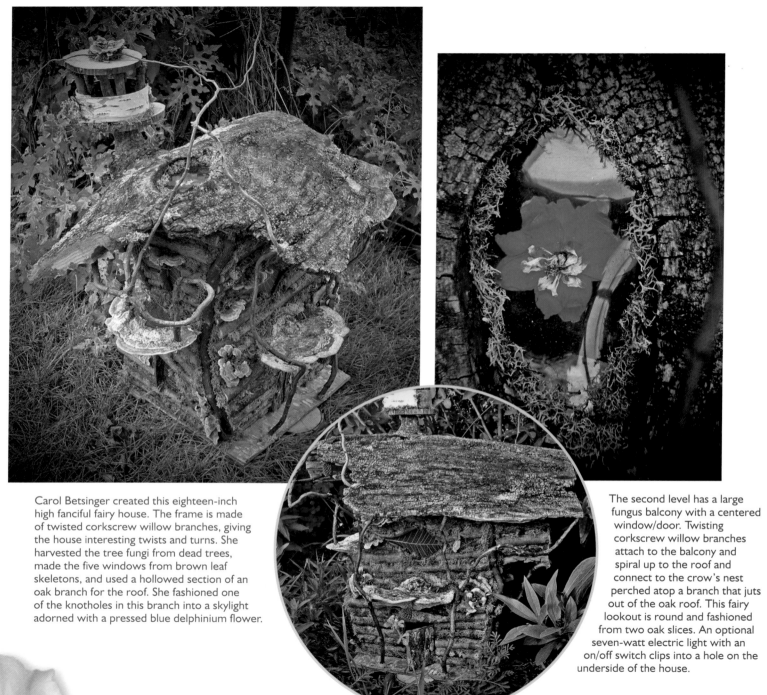

Carol Betsinger created this eighteen-inch high fanciful fairy house. The frame is made of twisted corkscrew willow branches, giving the house interesting twists and turns. She harvested the tree fungi from dead trees, made the five windows from brown leaf skeletons, and used a hollowed section of an oak branch for the roof. She fashioned one of the knotholes in this branch into a skylight adorned with a pressed blue delphinium flower.

The second level has a large fungus balcony with a centered window/door. Twisting corkscrew willow branches attach to the balcony and spiral up to the roof and connect to the crow's nest perched atop a branch that juts out of the oak roof. This fairy lookout is round and fashioned from two oak slices. An optional seven-watt electric light with an on/off switch clips into a hole on the underside of the house.

Paula Malta designed a welcoming rustic gazebo filled with the essentials that every tranquil garden room needs. A wreath of mini dried roses and a little mushroom bird greet the visitor. An inviting Victorian-style wire chair has a yo-yo pillow, and a straw hat with ribbon roses and satin ribbon bow waits to cover a head. The turtle wind chimes ring in the gentle breezes, a *Better Homes and Gardens* magazine rest on the table with two garden tools, two painted wood pots, shells, and a vase of lavender. And for companionship, there is a porcelain tabby kitty! *Courtesy of Elisa L. Harvey.*

Designed by Dani Mendenhall of Dragonfly Hollow, this fairy garden, entitled "Snow Day," began with a red tin bucket. The red hypoestes plants pull together the colors of the container with the red sled; the crushed white glass looks like a fresh snowfall. Add in the reindeer crossing sign with the snowman and the twinkling lights — and you are ready for a winter. This garden uses plants that can thrive indoors: gold selaginella, wax leaf ivy, and red hypoestes.
Courtesy of Kellen G. Peterson.

Sally J. Smith shaped daffodil cottages from living daffodil flowers and leaves in situ. When done, she leaves them there for the fairies to enjoy.
Courtesy of Sally J. Smith/ Greenspirit Arts.

Jay O'Rourke made this multi-layer pot for a garden show. The fairies love playing hide and seek under the mushrooms and enjoy sitting out on the patio. *Courtesy of Barbara Purchia.*

Roxie Zwicker cleaned and oven dried a pumpkin shell at a low temperature to create the roof on this simple, five-inch high autumn abode. Flat driftwood creates the floor, which is mounted to a wooden base. The two pillars of the house are thick pieces of driftwood branches. Silk flowers and fall berries are accents. A round wooden disc is covered in birch bark. On the table is a wand made from glass beads surrounded by orange gemstones.

Elaine England's outdoor fairy garden provides shelter as well as many colorful stones, feathers, and seashells. Lemon thyme is a favorite plant of welcome to fairies. The turtle is just about to enter the fairy's home. *Courtesy of Barbara Purchia.*

Sally J. Smith created a Birchwood House from white birch bark, golden birch, and white cedar branches. Poppyseed finials top the removable roofs. The house has several bay windows and a special tower room. Fully finished on the inside with micro LED lighting, this fairy house is magical at night. *Courtesy of Sally J. Smith/Greenspirit Arts.*

Simon Sinkinson of Tiny Doors for Tiny Things knows that his doors lead to safe havens for tiny things.

Sheryl Lozier of Summers Past creates a whimsical log home with animals, a vegetable garden, and strawberry field.
Courtesy of Whitbeck Photography, San Diego, CA.

29

This Moonlight Harvest garden, designed by Dani Mendenhall of Dragonfly Hollow, features a fairy kneeling while harvesting in the moonlight. The scene also includes a Sally Wilson gazing ball, mushroom seats, garden harvest tools, and harvest vegetables. *Courtesy of Kellen G. Peterson.*

Sally J. Smith made this colorful tea-house from a tulip, daffodils, and red fiddlehead fronds. She pinned it together with hawthorn thorns and nestled it in a dwarf rhododendron. *Courtesy of Sally J. Smith/Greenspirit Arts.*

Sheryl Lozier of Summers Past found a small green-painted chair to be a perfect home for fairies. A fairy forest of purple cabbage surrounds it.
Courtesy of Whitbeck Photography, San Diego, CA.

31

Sally J. Smith fashioned a purple tent from irises. This regal tent is for the queen! *Courtesy of Sally J. Smith/Greenspirit Arts.*

The Meadow Fairy who lives in this house designed by Tatiana Katara loves to change the location of her residence. In the summer, when it's warm and sunny, her house is out in the open. As winter approaches, she moves it to a protected spot in the woods, among the rocks and trees. Bits of cattail leaves frame the windows, and pine bark shingles the house. Tatiana points out that you should never use green materials for building because you could easily harm the plant or tree.

Lynsey Higginson describes her Vine Cottage as a great little property — perfect for newlyweds who are considering starting a family. Based deep in the woodlands, the cottage is close to other fairy dwellings, and a local fairy tavern is a short walk away.

All the wood Alison Barry and Brian Main use for their fairy houses is found washed up on riverbanks. They dry the wood, carefully hollow it out with doors and windows, and make an appropriate size roof and stand. They construct roof structures, doors, and window frames from twigs. Most of their houses have built-in lofts with illuminated stained glass windows in wooden or clay window frames. Internal LEDs bring their houses into life at night. Many even have a potted toadstool outside!

Lynsey's Ivy Heights is a beautiful woodland home for the more discerning fairy customer with a family. It occupies a large tree stump and has four large bedrooms and all the modern conveniences while still retaining its rustic character.

Beth Witsik constructed Claddagh House from a wood birdhouse stained a rich walnut and mounted on a tree stump. Her house is roofed in moss and trimmed with tree bark, dried flowers, acorns, and pine cones. The rear wall of the house is custom-fitted with a beautiful stained glass window. Wood, moss, fabric, acorns, and a birthday candle furnish the interior. You don't need to go to the end of the rainbow to find a pot of gold at Claddagh House.

Beth Powell points out that this cabin located between two popular destinations has four-star accommodations. Stocked with food and drink, the lobby/office offers a workspace with a desk and complimentary "wiFly." There is a porch off the downstairs room, which houses an aviary filled with exotic birds. Upstairs has a potbelly stove, a large bookcase, chair, a porch and an amazing view. The garden has a small wading pond for the weary travelers and stairs that lead up to a sitting deck overlooking the meadows. Picnics are enjoyed by the side of the pond, or upstairs on the deck. *Courtesy of Buffy Pollack.*

Built from natural woods and painted to complement the fall season, Art Millican's Tinkers Tree house finds itself right at home in a farmer's field.

Rob Heard's inspiration comes from the rolling countryside surrounding his home, where each Bough House sculpture takes several months to construct. His designs do not follow an explicit plan or process; rather, each piece evolves and flows freely, as part of a creative journey that has no natural limit, revealing great logic and engineering integrity. Every aerial walkway or staircase leads to a room — there are no dead ends — and every turret and tower can be reached.

Sally J. Smith was invited to create a special fairy garden display for the Vermont Flower Show in 2009. Part of her display was this fairy garden gazebo. *Courtesy of Sally J. Smith/Greenspirit Arts.*

This fairy gardener has been busy! Miniature work boots, garden tools, and a green bicycle sit just outside of this garden oasis designed by Mare Faulds. A mini garden, a luncheon table with a leaf teapot and botanical umbrella, and a hand-crafted potter's bench surround this garden scene.

Derrien Kilsby and Terry Severinski designed Wonky#2, with a cedar shingle roof, an over-sized door, and a chunky window frame. A large blue glass marble catches the sunlight, while the slightest breeze causes the bell, hanging from the tip of the roof, to tinkle, calling the other spirits. *Photo by Jenny Skopliak.*

Fairies in the Woodlands

2

When you are in the woods, you might look for signs from the fairies. Perhaps it is a wonderful acorn cap or a ring of mushrooms or the perfect flower. Little pieces of nature will become much more significant as you begin thinking about making a fairy house.

Linda Haas warns us to watch out for low-flying fairies because they always gather around the tree roots in her garden. She is always on the lookout for fun plants to add to her fairy garden. Notice the whimsical looking begonia called "Escargot." The fence and arbor are made from birch twigs.

The Dragonfly House by Sally J. Smith is a private commission. The front door is constructed with transparent films, which have been printed with images of actual dragonfly wings. They glow pinkish-purple when lit from behind. The wall sconce lights are faceted amber beads hanging below acorns, which have been hollowed out to hold a LED light. The windows are made from the same laminated layers as the door. The stone steps pull out to reveal the battery pack that powers the micro LED lighting.
Courtesy of Sally J. Smith/Greenspirit Arts.

Carol Betsinger created this fairy house to enthrall and stimulate the imagination of the young and old. Its rear is exposed for play. The first floor is the living area. The spiral staircase made from ½-inch slices of a dead peach branch and a willow wisp banister lead to the second floor bedroom. The bedroom's slanted ceiling has a circular skylight featuring a pressed swallowtail butterfly protected between two layers of clear acrylic. Notched and assembled log cabin style, the house is made with fallen limbs from such woodland trees as oak, maple, and ash. Moss fills the crevices. Stone steps lead to the front porch of white paper birch overlaid on thin plywood. The front door, also overlaid with birch bark, is attached with shiny gold hinges and opens and closes with a golden doorknob. Twisted corkscrew willow posts attach the porch to the roof overhang, which is lined with oak bark, a sacred tree to woodland fairies. The five windows have panes made from brown leaf skeletons. Carol used pinecone scales to shingle the house. Since fairies are particularly attracted to shiny colorful objects, she used broken pieces of china to grout the chimney.

Tori Carpenter made a woodland house of two floors encircled by an ancient bonsai weeping cherry tree. It includes a fishpond, sunflower garden, and root cellar full of goodies. If you look very closely, you might see the tiny fairy footprints along the garden path. The main lights are all tiny LEDs on two circuits: one for the interior and one for the exterior of the house. The chandelier, wall sconces, and carriage light are all formed into tiny candles and carefully detailed with paint. The fireplace includes a separate switch and features a vintage hardware chimney pipe. *Courtesy of Kevin Stevens*.

In Tree Secrets, Roxie Zwicker portrays her version of a fairy house inside of a tree. She shaped several pieces of pine tree bark to create a tree trunk and built the house on a large sheet of birch bark that had been flattened and placed on top of a plywood base. She added an abandoned bird's nest as a focal point. The two beds are made from dried rose petals and dried English ivy leaves. Fluffy feathers are used as pillows. Milkweed fluff can be found throughout the house, giving motion to the scene. The kitchen features a driftwood broom and shelves with dried seeds and flowers. Acorn top bowls contain dried oat tops, dried rose hips, lavender flowers, cloves, and marigold petals. The front door of the house is made from driftwood and features a grapevine wreath on the door. Nearby is a little garden full of crystals, dried strawflowers, and grasses.

Sally found a large shelf fungus, which
became the roof for the entrance. She
wove weeping willow twigs into two hoops
to make the windows and added a small
dormer window to the "roof." She used
some curved cedar branches as additional
decorative supports for the porch roof.
Courtesy of Sally J. Smith/Greenspirit Arts.

These moss-covered cliffs and boulder inspired
Sally J. Smith to build an Emerald Moss House. It
took her several days to collect and bring in the
stones from a nearby brook.
Courtesy of Sally J. Smith/Greenspirit Arts.

The Woodland Fairy House created by Mike and Debbie Schramer is 5' x 4'. This house is filled with intricate detail and amazing and beautiful little creations. It has fourteen rooms all completely furnished with little chairs, beds, tables, dishes, books, sculptures, paintings, brooms, shoes made from nature…everything in nature you can imagine: driftwood, branches, roots, vines, twigs, leaves, moss, flowers, stones, shells, seaweed, kelp, leaf skeleton, wild grasses, herbs, pods, and the list goes on. Note that the bedroom has a phonograph. *Courtesy of ChristyMcCullough.com.*

Sally J. Smith's Shire Cottage is made from white cedar twigs, white and golden birch, and river stones provided by an adjacent mountain stream. Sally made the door, the windows, and small roof tower in the studio. Dry tree fungus protects the windows and roof of the tiny window tower. Wild flowers decorate the gardens and roof, and a stone path leads down the bank to the river. *Courtesy of Sally J. Smith/ Greenspirit Arts.*

This classic three-story brownstone-inspired building was located in the city for a short time, while the owners entertained the idea of becoming city slickers. Shortly thereafter, they moved from the city back to their favorite land in the remote countryside, where it remains to this day. Designed by Tatiana Katara, Birchwood Manor is adorned with flower petals, wood, sticks, and plaster stones. The inside is as immaculate as the exterior.

Derrien Kilsby and Terry Severinski used recycled cedar to build these "Magical Mushrooms," in a quiet woodland setting. The mushroom in the top right has a patchwork design of rough cedar squares. Top left shows a mushroom with a roof design of alternating dowelling and dark cedar strips. The center mushroom has a round door with dark cedar spots decorating the mushroom top. *Photo by Jenny Skopliak.*

Beth Witsik transformed a log cabin planter into the Post Cabin. She decorated the new moss roof with pinecones, dried mushrooms, acorns, and a honeycomb. The rustic interior has an Altoid tin bed filled with soft moss, a sofa, feather rug, baskets, tables, pixie dust, and sparkling Christmas lights. She provided additional space through a front porch featuring a stick ladder, bronze bell, lounge chair, two acorn sconces, and a honeycomb. To add to fairy fun, she made a tire swing.

The twists and turns of four corner cork-screw willow branches shape this house made by Carol Betsinger. The walls of the house are built with fallen tree branches, cut into "logs," with green moss filling in the cracks. The oak bark front door and second-story balcony door have golden doorknobs and tiny gold hinges that open and close. Gold-dyed leaf skeletons are used as windowpanes. The inside is carpeted with a natural blanket of lush green moss.

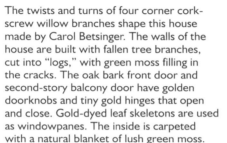

The roof is fashioned from a section of hollowed tree trunk with moss and lichen. Three different varieties of tree fungus adorn the windows, doors, and exterior walls. Black Hills pinecones are suspended from the roof's overhang. The dried purple lavender "growing" around the base of the house and on the second floor of the balcony will surely attract the lavender fairies!

49

Tatiana Katara's little birch cottage looks like it came straight from *Grimm's Fairy Tales*.

The birch tree spirits are known to be very benevolent beings. Here, the birch trees surround this Tatiana Katara home, which blends in easily with its environs.

Sally J. Smith transformed a large moss-covered stump into a magical palace for forest fairies. She gathered all elements in this house from the immediate area.
Courtesy of Sally J. Smith/Greenspirit Arts.

Derrien Kilsby and Terry Severinski give us an array of houses: The Sue, Mini Wonk, and the Mushroom.

Refurbished wind chimes hang playfully from the roof edge of The Sue, while the door opens outward on over-sized hinges. The open bottom allows for placement over an unsightly tree stump. *Photo by Derrien Kilsby.*

Mini Wonk, the smallest of the garden cottages, is accented with steel ball bearings, silver upholstery studs and a chrome doorknob. A small mirror set inside a wooden toy wheel acts as a window.
Photo by Jenny Skopliak.

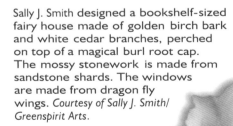

Mushroom adds whimsy to any garden. An aquamarine-colored glass ball is embedded in the wood.
Photo by Jenny Skopliak.

Sally J. Smith designed a bookshelf-sized fairy house made of golden birch bark and white cedar branches, perched on top of a magical burl root cap. The mossy stonework is made from sandstone shards. The windows are made from dragon fly wings. *Courtesy of Sally J. Smith/ Greenspirit Arts.*

Beth Witsik constructed this fairy cottage from a chicken wire cage and nestled it into a magnificent piece of driftwood. The roof is covered in tropical seedpods, Spanish moss, and rope. Seashells and coral collected from around the world accent the perimeter. Inside seashells, sea glass, sewing spools, miniatures, polymer clay, rope, marble, fabric, and potpourri are used to make the furniture and accessories. The interior is decorated in shades of blue, ivory, and brown. The coconut shell club chair is a cozy spot to curl up after a long day in the sun.

Fairies Along the Water

The many water fairies range from Undines to Kelpies. Their homes are typically within rocky or coral pools, lakes, and ponds or along the banks of rivers. Some smaller fairies may choose to live under lily pads.

Derrien Kilsby and Terry Severinski give us some fishing shacks. Beautiful Whonnock Lake in British Columbia is a backdrop to this fishing shack with its brightly-colored, wooden fish moving gently in the breeze. Sunlight bathes the rocks and highlights the charm of this fishing shack. Copper mesh acts as a windowpane, and recycled fishing tackle and hardware decorate the porch. Randomly placed cedar shingles adorn the roof of this recycled rough cedar cottage. Fishing weights and swivels dangle from the windowsill. The top eyelet of a well-used fishing rod works nicely as a door handle.
Photos by Jenny Skopliak and Derrien Kilsby.

Fairies have unlimited and wonderful housing opportunities, so they are known to be a transient bunch. Working with a master architect, Beth Powell fashioned this Green Home using driftwood from the surrounding environs. When this house was completed, several sites were tried out until it was positioned on Faerie Beacon Rock. This home has a back-to-the-basics summer kitchen with a large fire pit with a cauldron always cooking some delicious meal. A staircase leads to the door of this small home from the beach below. Because the builder of this home used all local materials, it can withstand all kinds of weather. *Courtesy of Buffy Pollack.*

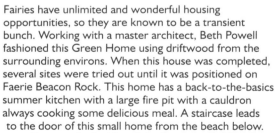

Emily Crooker built Careyes Cottage for a family in Mexico. Its residents have a beautiful ocean view and a pinecone roof. The centerpiece of tropical bird feathers complements the shell plates and coral silverware. *Courtesy of Enchanted Gourds.*

55

Paula Malta made a magical retreat with natural branches, vines, and grasses and filled it with shells, a shell brush, sumptuous fabric, vintage buttons, and other accessories she couldn't live without. Of course, she has "fire-flies" to illuminate her beautiful surroundings at night through battery-operated LED lights. Inside her cozy retreat is a fairy bed made with cinnamon sticks, bark, tiny shells, pink quartz beads, covered with luxurious designer fabric and tiny lace trim, a pillow covered with tiny faux roses and a scalloped shell headboard that glitters.

Dani Mendenhall's Day at the Shore is designed to evoke pleasant memories of time spent at the seashore and lazy days along the beach. *Courtesy of Susan Peterson.*

Tatiana Katara built a fairy castle in the sand.

Beth Powell designed a contemporary home for a water fairy.
Courtesy of Buffy Pollack.

Art Millican built a teapot castle along the water. Perched on a driftwood stump, this little brass house sits at the edge of a quiet stream. The use of brass and wood gives it a nautical look while the green patina from the aging of the brass helps it blend into the tall river weeds.

Sally J. Smith used dry-laid stones gathered from the river to construct Riverstone Tower. A spiral garden adorns the roof while a delicate stone stairway rises over a pothole pool to a simple door in this large tower house. *Courtesy of Sally J. Smith/Greenspirit Arts.*

Beach fairies adore large seashells as they are perfect building material. Roxie Zwicker built this house from driftwood and large seashells. A large scallop shell is the roof. Soft green reindeer moss cascades down the walls and around the corners of the house. She made a little table from a seashell mounted to a piece of coral and sprinkled herbs on it.

Fairies' delight when Beth Powell's *S.S. Serendipity* arrives! With snakeskin sails and a sleek physique, this ship flies with the wind over fields, through forests, and across oceans, but also stops in accordance to its passengers' whims, allowing fairies to disembark. Space is always at a premium on the *S.S. Serendipity*. The quarterdeck features a hot tub and an outdoor fire pit under the shadows of the sail with little fairy seats perched above it for warmth. The deck is a cork-floored "floating" dance floor, with a popular stage (a waiting list even!) and bar renowned for its famous cocktails. The Captain's Quarters is equipped with another fire pit, where the Captain and his friends can roll the dice to determine their next sailing destination. A celestial globe will set the course. The bow houses a private room, obtained by lottery, and a grill above for that midnight snack. This ship is protected from evil by the Woodskuls, carved skull totems that live above the sails and ward off harm. Very popular indeed, the *S.S. Serendipity*. *Courtesy of Buffy Pollack.*

Emily Crooker gives us Under The Sea, home to our New England seashore water fairy. It is covered with barnacles and decorated with shells. *Courtesy of Enchanted Gourds.*

61

John Crawford's "The Accidental Wizard" is a three-foot-tall, four-level masterpiece, fully furnished and detailed to accommodate the strange and slightly scattered lifestyle of a brilliant but fumbling wizard named Alberic. Each floor has a piece of wall that opens to allow human friends to peek at the interior space. This masterful creation sits on an octagonal floor stand in a bay window with enough room for curious viewers to roam around all sides. There are interior lights sufficient for Alberic's purposes, but a flashlight sits near the house to give visitors a better view of the minute details of the interior. ©*Fairy Woodland.*

The house reflects the curious wizard who inhabits it, tipping its "head" to the side trying to puzzle out the answer to a new question. The roof has a scattering of strange objects, which include a telescope and a lightning rod. The large prominence on the right side is a driftwood piece outside the wizard's bedroom window that resembles a dragon. Perhaps it is singing to the stars. In his fourth-floor observatory, the fairy wizard uses his telescope to search the heavens for patterns that are reflected on earth. ©*Fairy Woodland.*

Fairy Tales and Creatures

4

Many supernatural creatures dot our world, particularly when we are children: the fairy godmothers who act as mentors, the trolls of Scandinavia, the Seven Dwarfs, Tinker Belle in *Peter Pan*, the leprechauns of the Irish, and the many other generally invisible elves, pixies, and mermaids who have populated our fairy tales, myths, and legends. They are generally grouped under the umbrella term "fairy."

Every chapter on fairy tales needs a few castles for ambitious fairies and their growing families. Rob Heard gets inspired by a tree bough cut from local trees or found lying in the fields. He allows the shape and twists of the branch to inform his design.

Mare Faulds transformed a faux apple into a quaint woodland gourmet apple shop. Iridescent green rocks pave the entrance. Miniature caramel apples are displayed on a leaf-covered woodland cart outside. Sparkly interior walls surround a mini wood table displaying more of the delicious looking apples. A botanical ladder reaches a balcony with a set of table and chairs, awaiting the fairies that want more of a "scenic view" while enjoying their treats.

64

Sally J. Smith's Dragon Fairy House was inspired by a piece of driftwood that now forms the arching "Dragon" guarding the front door. All the roofs, including the ivy leaf-covered main roof, are removable. Garden poppy seed heads form the finials of the roofs. The front door is hinged with birch twigs, which look like crow's feet. Two quartz crystal lamps grace the stone stairs. The crystals glow when dusk falls. Each window is glazed with transparent "Faerie Film" and peeled white cedar twigs. *Courtesy of Sally J. Smith/ Greenspirit Arts.*

Children immediately want to play with Margot van de Wiel's felting scenes. Here, little animals want to play hide-and-seek in the trees.

This house, called Reach for the Sky, embodies John Crawford's quest to bring to life the animate nature of the twigs and stones from which his houses are made. Some fairy houses sit firmly on the ground; this one leaps from its base, seemingly dancing in thin air. Cedar roots are a favorite medium because they force the shape of the walls into the contorted, twisted forms that make his sculpture really interesting. ©Fairy Woodland.

This house is about joy and freedom. Each view of the house is an element of its choreography. The keeper of the house has placed it at the edge of a large picture window where it can watch the trees in the surrounding forest dance with the winds. The gestural quality of the twigs leaves the impression that this house is running on four legs while standing upright. It holds a magical stone in its upraised acorn cup hand. As the light changes through the course of the day and night, the gestural quality of the twigs describe a dance of exuberance. It leaps…It bows…It reaches as though offering a hand to a partner in the dance. ©*Fairy Woodland*.

Art Millican built an enchanted castle in the frozen lands of the ice fairies. Tall, regal towers grace the stone gardens.

Sally J. Smith titled this "Home of the Winter Sun." Constructed entirely of ice gathered from a frozen lake, this Ice Castle stands over six feet tall. It was oriented so that the light of the solstice sunset would illuminate the sculpture from behind. *Courtesy of Sally J. Smith/Greenspirit Arts.*

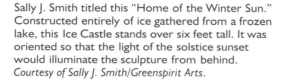

Mare Faulds transformed a wooden birdhouse using a texture technique, brown and black paint, and faux tree branches. This darker style fairy house is the home of the Unseelie fairy queen. She has her wood-stemmed chair with her headdress that awaits her. Inside there is a path of burnt-on tribal markings and an altar with her spell book and skull candle. A hand-crafted enchanted tree trunk was made from paper clay.

Mike and Debbie Schramer created this fairy castle from natural and found materials from the woods, sea, meadows, fields, and gardens. It is about two feet tall; filled with many rooms and furniture, books, dishes, paintings, sculptures, and many other fantastic details. Notice the charming laundry and dining rooms.
Courtesy ChristyMcCullough.com.

The gnarly driftwood pieces that form the structure for this John Crawford creation feature faces and shapes of a flock of otherworld characters. When the full moon hits the fused glass dais suspended in the center of the house and is reflected onto the blown glass swirl on the floor, the myriad creatures locked in the wood come to life and roam the premises. The snowflake-shaped platform that hovers in space is the focal point for the interior of this piece. A fused glass artist created this magical gateway specifically for this project. The lens at the center of the snowflake guides the moonlight to the floor. ©Fairy Woodland.

Tatiana Katara built this palace, using cut-up grapevine strips, old plaster from a demolished house, a tiny thrift store basket, air-dry clay, flowers, mushrooms, an old curtain, a bit of lace, and glue. A pink flower marks the balcony — can't you imagine Rapunzel standing here?

Mare Faulds created Jak's Beanstalk Bed & Breakfast in an extra large dense packing tube that has been lightly textured and painted with multiple shades of green paint. The oversized deep green leaves that wrap around the structure are perfect to fit the hand-crafted flower fairies that are nestled in for a good night's sleep. The display includes a "fly in" outdoor shower and leafy bunk beds.

Avery, shown here, is a messenger fairy, and you can often find her carrying her bottle of messages through the woods.

Sandy Darling hand-sculpts various fairies from high quality polymer clay over a strong wire armature. The arms are jointed at the shoulder and can move freely.

Emmie, the Critter Whisperer, is a shy, playful little fairy with a heart of gold. Emmie is famous for her ability to nurse injured animals back to health.

Fairies use totems and other symbols to ward off evil around their environs. Designed by Beth Powell, these enemies of the Fae were caught by a trip wire camera in Southern Oregon. Feared mostly in the rugged Southern Oregon coastal mountain range communities, they have been suspected of visiting Rogue Valley looking for unsuspecting victims from time to time. *Courtesy of Buffy Pollack.*

Linda Haas from Tree Star Hollow designed a fairy house using a stump from a dead apple tree. She made the stained glass windows, cut each door, and hand painted them.

Using natural materials found in the woods, Art Millican's dwarf cottage brings a childhood story to life.

This wee fairy scene by David Rau is based on "Chapter 20: The Dainty China Country" in L. Frank Baum's 1900 masterpiece, *The Wonderful Wizard of Oz*. In the story, Dorothy and her friends climb over a wall to find a world where the houses, people, and animals are all made of porcelain. The mixed media assemblage is on a wood and ceramic base. *Courtesy of Tammi Flynn.*

A collector commissioned John Crawford to make this Fairydontist office for her orthodontist husband. Notice the "telescope" on the roof, which funnels light to the second-floor operating room. *Note: Interior views of this structure can be found on pages 78 and 79.*

Fairies in the Community

5

Fairies, gnomes, undines, sylphs, and other nature spirits are considered by many to be spirits within our world. They are believed to be fine gold and silversmiths and excellent metalworkers. They own cattle and have dogs. They grow plants and vegetables and collect fruits for living.

© Fairy Woodland

The Fairydontist office serves fairies, elves, gnomes, nymphs, sprites, and ogres (by appointment only). No toads, however. The first-floor waiting room is complete with appointment book, patient files spilling chaotically out of the shelves, and magazines for patients to read.
©Fairy Woodland.

The second-floor examining area includes a dentist chair for fairy patients and a crane for holding open the mouths of large creatures, such as dragons. ©*Fairy Woodland*.

Nestled in the dried grass, overlooking a valley, looms a large fairy commune, nicknamed Shangri La. This palatial commune was the brainchild of Beth Powell and a fairy who wanted to provide a healthy and cohesive housing alternative for fairies. They discovered an old Saguaro cactus shell, which made a perfect foundation for the commune, while carved-out gourds provided dwellings inside of dwellings. *Courtesy of Buffy Pollack.*

In keeping with the communal spirit, this community has common areas in the way of decks connected with Oriental-carpeted hallways, staircases, and ladders. In the popular nursery, matrons lovingly nurture the fairy children while their parents spend their time working or frolicking. *Courtesy of Buffy Pollack.*

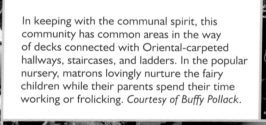

The Gourd Nursery, on the left, is where the babies sleep in miniature beds covered in silk. On the right, another gourd provides small rooms with a common gathering place at the top of the home inside this gourd. The South End is where residents meet around the fire to hold council and make new friends.
Courtesy of Buffy Pollack.

The steampunk genre inspired Roxie Zwicker to build this large, two-story house. Steampunk is a stylized industrial-inspired art form that features steam-powered machinery during the Victorian period. This house is for the fairies who like something other than gardens or woodlands.

The fairies who live here have made the most of uncommon items. The house frame is largely made from dried pine bark and apple tree branches from a 200-year-old orchard, brass connectors from a 1950s machine have become tables and windows, and the floor is a collection of papers, letters, and charts from the 1930s.

The front of the house features several clock faces, an old rusty wall hook, and a small mirror mounted to the walls. Charts of fantastic flying machines from the nineteenth century hang in the inside of the ceiling and walls. Roxie left lichens and chips in the wood on the branches to make them appear old. She stacked pieces like blocks to give the house a more artificial feel.

The decks around the trunk of the tree were built with pilfered embroidery hoops, using a bamboo place mat for flooring. A hut was placed above and turned into the loft. The stage lighting is dried flowers turned upside down. *Courtesy of Buffy Pollack.*

Built into a ficus plant, the Fairy Music Venue showcases a cornucopia of talent. It was conceived by Beth Powell and a fairy architect who, on the side, is a banjo player for a popular fairy band known throughout the region. His concept was to build a venue that would take musicians' comfort and well being to a new level. The loft above the main stage has hammocks, a sink area/wash basin area, table and chairs, and a desk with an inflatable oak gall ball seat. The 360-degree views from the loft within the high branches of this tree give musicians a quiet place to reflect before the show. The main stage is set for a three-piece Blue Grass band.

Simon Sinkinson envisions the fairies building a plane.

Beth Witsik designed a Fairy Delicious Bakery. She used a decorative iron birdcage wrapped in vines of artificial leaves, berries, and pink cherry blossoms mounted onto a round tree stump and wood, gingham cupcake liners, and sewing spools for the tables on the outside patio.

Inside, polymer clay, miniatures, sugar, artificial flowers and leaves created the sweets and accessories for serving. As the local fairies know, there is no better place to sip a cup of tea from a flower petal cup than at one of tables set with cupcake liner tablecloths. Homemade pastries, pies, cakes, cookies, tarts, and bread are artfully arranged on the counter, baker's cabinet, and the circular shelf that runs along the interior of the roof.

83

Beth Powell knows that majestic oaks are a four-star destination for fairy travelers. On the left of this hanging hostel is the suite, made inviting by a sheepskin rug and lush pillows. Below on the main deck is a candle-lit communal dining area, a fire pit, and access to an outdoor sitting room. There is plenty of room for dancing, of course, which begins at twilight each evening. Stairs lead to the main hostel with plenty of welcoming rooms. The round dome at the top of this house is actually a planter. The architects chose this spot as they envisioned additional summer shade as a plant grew down and around this hostel. An inverted branch from an oak supports the large main deck, which became the foundation for the rest of the structure. *Courtesy of Buffy Pollack.*

Mare Faulds' fairy wedding scene has pink and purple elements, a sparkly, rock-edged wood base, and an enchanted dress that looks as if the doves are flying it to the bride. The wedding table has been set with six leaf chairs, real miniature rose petals as confetti, candles, and a flower centerpiece. The pink coordinating carriage is made from botanical bowl filler and transformed with pink flowers and bits of botanicals. The grounds have trees, a birdbath, and a hand-crafted cake table that has a miniature wedding cake, a champagne bottle, and two glasses. Cheers!

Fairies and Special Occasions

6

Fairies like special occasions. They enjoy decorating for a party, planning wonderful food, and dancing to great music.

Beth Pomroy created the wedding chapel with presents waiting to be opened.

Even snail parties can become somewhat unruly. Simon Sinkinson created a beautiful "Thank You" cake with drinks and cookies. The snails really enjoyed it!

Designed for a truly patriotic fairy who visits a little girl whose father was serving overseas, Beth Witsik's Red, White and Blue Cottage overflows with sentimental and personal touches. It is the perfect house for a fairy whose mission is watching over an airman's daughter each night. Inside there are two floors of spacious living filled with daily reminders of a Dad serving his country, including a framed squadron insignia and a yellow ribbon on the front door. The eat-in kitchen, complete with a stove and seashell sink, is stocked with everything needed to prepare a home-cooked meal.

An earring chandelier and Grandma's linen handkerchiefs helped create this sweet bedroom underneath a ceiling that is painted with both the day and night skies!

Beth Pomroy's made a Valentine's Dinner for Michelle from a salvaged plank base, twigs, polymer clay, handmade paper, beads, and shells. The table is set with statice flowers, bead wineglasses, shell plates, bark paper tablecloth, and a polymer clay bucket with a carved wax champagne bottle.

Emily Crooker celebrates Halloween with the Spider King fairy house. A throne crafted from a king crab shell and black ostrich feathers serves as the royal seat for the Spider King. *Courtesy of Enchanted Gourds.*

Fairies have taken over the spooky old barn to hold a neighborhood Halloween party with yummy treats, games, and a gleaming gourd jack-o-lantern. All lighting is created using tiny LEDs wired to one switch and battery. Tori Carpenter used wood, clay, moss, paint, fabric, paper, sticks, industrial GID paint, and spiderwebs! *Courtesy of Kevin Stevens.*

Emily Crooker hung her stockings with care in this fairy house charmingly decorated for Christmas. *Courtesy of Enchanted Gourds*.

John Crawford created this twelve-foot fairy holiday extravaganza as a Christmas lobby display. This is Santa's home and the factory in which the fairies and elves make toys. The meandering village street features shops of all sorts. The interior shot is of Santa's home. ©*Fairy Woodland*.

Emily Crooker's Woodland Study is home to a fairy botanist whose studies center on various fungi and tree bark. Topped with a vintage 1950s ornament, the study has a wall of birch bark and shelf mushrooms. Other than the resin stool, the interior is made entirely of natural mushrooms, bark, and seedpods. *Courtesy of Enchanted Gourds.*

Fairy Furniture and Decor

7

Perhaps fairies were the first recyclers. They often borrow from humans, transforming our trash into treasure.

Emily Crooker of Enchanted Gourds designed a "Stuga," which is Swedish for country home. She has a blue and white, hand-painted tile stove, a grandfather clock, stenciled walls, and driftwood floor. *Courtesy of Enchanted Gourds.*

Tori Carpenter presents two scenes involving wood stoves. In the first, a fairy kitty warms herself by the wood stove (actually heated using roses). The wall paintings are by www.cinderellamoments.com. The second gives us a perfect cozy spot for cooking and reading while it snows outside. *Courtesy of Kevin Stevens.*

Ginger Fuller created a sumptuous sitting room for a fairy.

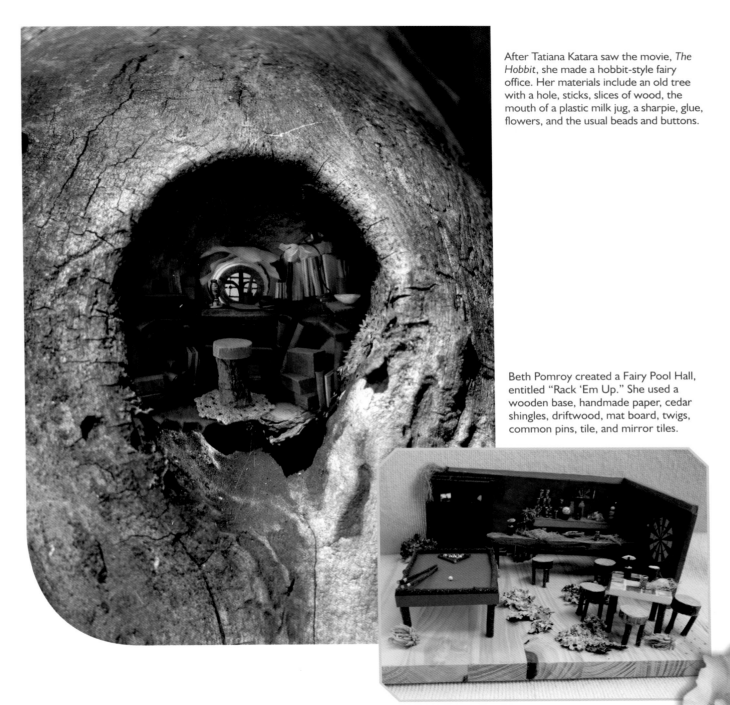

After Tatiana Katara saw the movie, *The Hobbit*, she made a hobbit-style fairy office. Her materials include an old tree with a hole, sticks, slices of wood, the mouth of a plastic milk jug, a sharpie, glue, flowers, and the usual beads and buttons.

Beth Pomroy created a Fairy Pool Hall, entitled "Rack 'Em Up." She used a wooden base, handmade paper, cedar shingles, driftwood, mat board, twigs, common pins, tile, and mirror tiles.

Inspired by Julia Child, Emily Crooker of Enchanted Gourds designed a fairy kitchen fully stocked for a gourmet meal. A recipe from the *Mastering the Art of French Cooking* is written on the exterior. The kitchen features a stove with French franc burners and a cinnamon stick hanging rack. *Courtesy of Enchanted Gourds.*

Tatiana Katara's rustic fairy kitchen features a tall window for the nature-loving fairy who wants that view. The cupboards and cabinets are made of weathered woodchips and the tiny drawer pulls are made from sliced-up sticks, split in half. A moss rug, acorn bowls, shell sink, finishing nail faucet, and twig plate rack help add charm to an otherwise simple country kitchen.

In this example of a rustic fairy kitchen, an eggshell sink sits under the graceful curving faucet, which is the end of a Devil's Claw tendril, as is the light hanger. The light fixture is made with twine and flowers.

Beth Pomroy designed a fairy luncheon from a spruce slab, twigs, sand dollars, pinecones, moss, shells, beads, acorn caps, and sea lavender. The drink umbrellas add a sense of playfulness to the scene!

Beth Powell created an intimate breakfast nook in an old log. *Courtesy of Buffy Pollack.*

Tatiana Katara's dining room really invites the outdoors in. It has the look and feel of a fairy forest, but if you look closely, you'll see that some of the walls are painted and then adorned with real bark to make them feel more real. The stone fireplace is used for cooking. A bottle cap is the saucepan; a cedar shake shingle is the table; the chairs are made from steak bones and topped with flat stones; and real moss carpets the floor.

97

Tori Carpenter created a Cupcake House for fairies who love sugar and sweets. Painted shabby pink and mint green, the house features handmade curtains, an operable window, a sparkling chandelier, artisan paintings, and "Chiclets" tiles.
Courtesy of Kevin Stevens.

Waking up in this gorgeous bedroom designed by Ginger Fuller is a delight for deserving fairies.

Who wouldn't want to sit on Tatiana Katara's stool cushioned in purple clover blossoms?

Doilies and red-striped linens, lace coverlets, and a Swedish Dala horse adorn this fairy bedroom fashioned by Emily Crooker. *Courtesy of Enchanted Gourds.*

Beth Pomroy has made two bedrooms for fairies. The first one uses birch and cedar bark, sand dollar, acorn caps, moss, beads, smooth stones, aluminum foil, sisal, and fabric. The rug is made from woven cornhusks. Note the painting on birch bark. The second uses birch bark, handmade paper, moss, twigs, acorn cap, old sweater, fabric, and polymer clay. Some of the details include the bark pants, twig cane, acorn cap beret, and the blanket made from an old sweater.

Emily Crooker made Wonderland for a book-loving little girl named Reena. It stands approximately 15" tall and sports walls papered with book pages and tiny pencils.
Courtesy of Enchanted Gourds.

For fairies that want a truly special night out, this private getaway offers peace and solitude in a garden setting with an outdoor bedroom concealed with mossed-over vines. This rustic, yet lavish room and garden was designed by one of the most well-known fairy designers of her day, Venus Fi, and her assistant Beth Powell. Music wafts through the air from the gramophone as guests enjoy an acre of paradise. There is a pond on the south end with a soft sandy bottom. Next to it is a shelter with a wide, smooth piece of driftwood for a bench. The fire pit is just outside this shelter in a patch of soft moss to sprawl out in. Fairy fires don't go out in rain or shine, so this place is fairy divine! A gravel path leads guests through the sands and back to the bedroom. Bullfrogs and owls join in the tranquility and lull their guests to sleep. In the morning, breakfast is served in bed! *Courtesy of Buffy Pollack.*

Beth Pomroy offsets her earth tones with accents from the seashore in her bathrooms. After all, shells make great bathtubs for diminutive fairies!

Beth Pomroy also created this charming outhouse using cedar shingles, twigs, shells, rocks, bark, and handmade paper. Note the handmade toilet paper rolls, the water-colored "girly" calendar, and the cleaning utensils.

Linda Haas designs comfortable chairs for a woodland setting.

Many fairy house designers illuminate their work. Here, we see two houses from Alison Barry and Brian Main illuminated by internal LEDs. The night comes alive with fairies and dramatic colors.

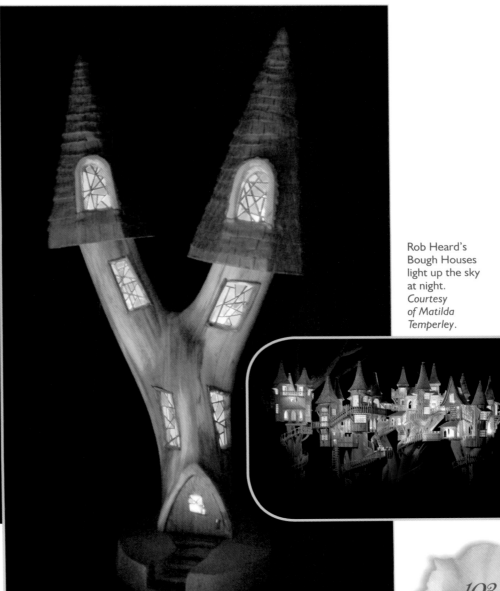

Rob Heard's Bough Houses light up the sky at night. *Courtesy of Matilda Temperley.*

103

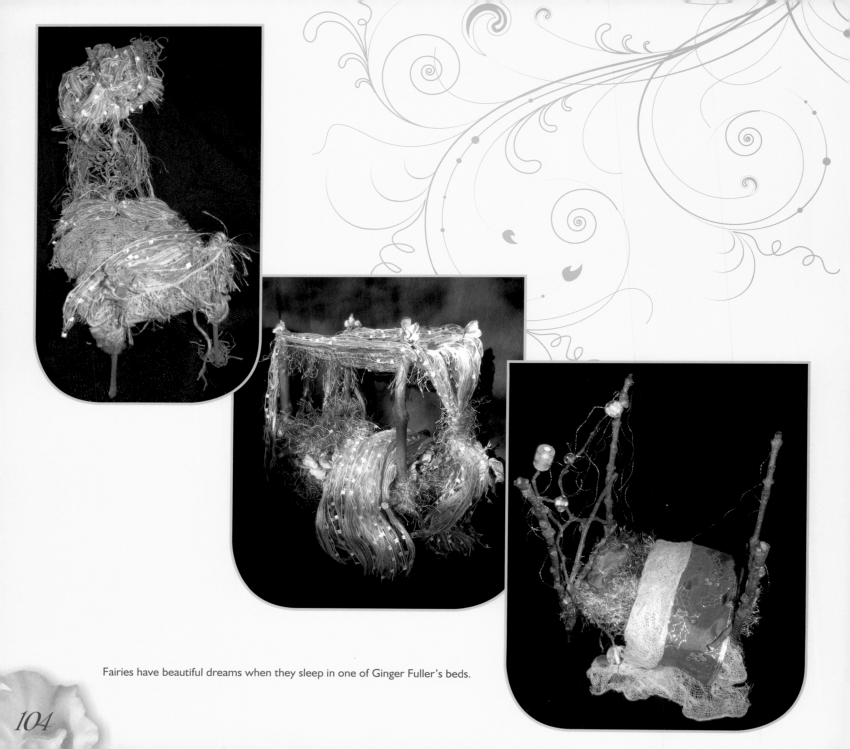

Fairies have beautiful dreams when they sleep in one of Ginger Fuller's beds.

Emily Crooker designed a peacock feather and twig bed for the Peacock Room. Courtesy of Enchanted Gourds.

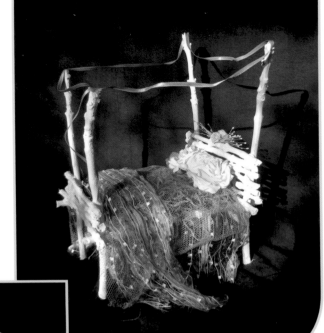

David Rau decorates his fairy-home doors with natural objects. *Courtesy of Al Malpa.*

Doors

Doorways can be pathways to new worlds. If we walk through a doorway, we may find that we can make a change by entering a new world.
The same is true for fairies.

Alison Barry and Brian Main make their fairy house doors from reclaimed oak with colored glass windows. They are illuminated from inside the house. Depending on their size, they have either a shaped (heart, moon, star, tree, etc.) window or colored-painted panel. The doors have brass knobs (some with a key!) and may also have letter-boxes and hinges.

Linda Haas of Tree Star Hollow designs and creates fairy houses and accessories using items collected from nature. She incorporates seed pods, dried flowers, and last season's grasses in her work.

Simon Sinkinson of Tiny Doors for Tiny Things points out that "Deep in the forest lie many tiny doors, the homes of the quietest, smallest, shyest creatures. As you amble through the woods, keep your eyes peeled for signs of tiny life — a little wooden wheelbarrow filled with acorns or a tiny napkin left after a fairy tea." His tiny doors are safe havens for tiny things.

Skyland Trail inspires adults with mental illness to thrive through a holistic program of evidence-based psychiatric treatment, integrated medical care, research and education. The phenomenon associated with young adults finding solace in fairy home-building and gardening parallels the goals set forth in horticultural therapy at Skyland Trail and the process of recovery: awe, empowerment, and connection, held together by hope.

Creating fairy homes and gardens is an integral part of recovery for adults with serious mental illness at Skyland Trail, a non-profit, community-based mental health treatment facility in Atlanta, Georgia. Initiated in 2006 by Susie Sherrill, PhD, LC, process art therapist at Skyland Trail, the activity soon took root in horticultural therapy, expanding to the therapeutic gardens and surrounding Atlanta community. Horticultural therapy at Skyland Trail is a goal-based adjunctive therapy, complementing verbal therapies, with a three-fold purpose: to enhance self-worth and self-esteem, to instill positive metaphors in recovery and relapse, and to provide connection through mindful and purposeful activities.

At Skyland Trail, fairy gardening and home-building are a collaboration between nature, the enchanting world of fairies, and the predominantly young adult clients engaged in the activity through horticultural therapy. "As children," Susie explains, "most of our young adult clients constructed with Lego blocks, which are linear and limiting. In fairy gardening, clients create in cooperation with nature, participating in the ecology of the natural world, whose process they begin to trust through experience; even when amorphous shapes come together in surprising ways, as they do in life."

Fairy gardening and home-building are also a collaboration with the journey of recovery of mental illness, especially in bipolar illness, through the unfold affirmation of oneself and one's potential, mirrored in the presence of nature. The process parallels the recovery journey from awe and reverence to empowerment and connection.

A*F*T*E*R*W*O*R*D

Fairy Gardening and Home-building as Therapy at Skyland Trail

LIBBA SHORTRIDGE, MLA, HTR

Throughout my six years as horticultural therapist at Skyland Trail, I am continually inspired by the adult clients with whom I work. By empowering clients in their recovery journey to embrace the creative world of fairy home-building and gardening, I, myself, am empowered. What began as an appreciation of nature in the therapeutic group called, "Nature as Healer," developed into an expansion of the gardens and an outreach into the community. The clients' engagement and enhanced self-esteem gave me impetus to write a grant to expand our gardens and therapeutic program to foster positive connections — both personal and social — through nature-inspired activities. A new therapeutic group was formed called, "Inspired by Nature," with the focus of creating fairy homes and gardens year-round. Fairy communities were created on two areas of the main campus where the talents and passions of clients could come to fruition on a miniature scale. In these communities, streams and lakes were formed; railroad tracks were laid alongside a beach and through pastures. A plane circled overhead where boats launched, while the labyrinth and Zen garden offered a place of respite. Woven fences made of *elaeagnus* whips protected the communities. Imagination, creativity, and fairies are welcomed here.

The fairy home is in us all
Something big in something small
Magic that is in our hearts
Can always become a work of art
A place to go and just escape
Let stress and sadness fade;
My fairy home is what I made.
~ by Kenia

Mobile magic / Moss so green / Wagon gardens / Built for fairy queens ...
Poem by Jenny M.; Jenny's and Margaret's fairy homes in a Red Flyer wagon.
Courtesy of Kathryn Rogers.

HOPE GENERATES HEALING

"Involving clients in a microcosm of the world empowers them to successfully create, thus raising their self-esteem and preparing them for success in the full-sized world," Susie Sherrill explains. One client reflects on the benefits of working in the miniature scale with fairies in mind, "There is so much bigness that we cannot control. It is nice to have something that is not overwhelming."

Things from nature — and in our own lives — taken for granted suddenly have multiple, fascinating uses. The fuzzy seed pod of a wisteria vine can become a sofa for fairies or a column for their home. When opened, the seed pod curls to become a spiral staircase for fairies to climb. The simple acorn cap in a fairy home, made from a coir pot, can become a chimney, a sink, a mailbox, or a pillow, filled with the downy seed of butterfly weed. "The process was a lot of fun," Allison writes about building her fairy home with the acorn top that held down the sheaths of silver dollar seeds. "I could be creative and imaginative, which is a side of myself that I've just started exploring." For Jenny, the creation of a "fairyland" in a Red Flyer wagon was a freeing experience. "I feel like I have glitter in my hair again...I'm rediscovering simple beauty and uncovering misplaced whimsy," she said.

The process of seeing things in nature with new meaning gives the clients a sense of hope and possibility. Tony relates his experience of creating his "Misty Mountain Fairies" as one that was "challenging and exciting...I was like a child again, discovering a new world." In the process of creating, Tony wrote, "I always found myself smiling and enjoying just 'that' moment...like children do..." Heather wrote about her experience, "My favorite part was letting the fairy home take shape on its own. Once I was able to let go of the idea of perfection, building the fairy home became very therapeutic and meditative. I found joy in the moment and lost track of time." The practice of being mindfully in the present and without judgment is reiterated in the dialectical behavioral therapy (DBT) skills that many clients, including Tony and Heather, are engaged in at Skyland Trail.

Uncovering Misplaced Whimsy

When I was little, I'd sprinkle glitter in my hair and twirl around the backyard pretending to be Pippi Longstocking or perhaps Maria from *The Sound of Music*. Those role models emanated joy and exuded insouciance. I'm still drawn to glittery shoes and nail polish, but I lost some of the fairy-tale fantasy in growing up.

I became the kind of artist who would plan out itemized lists of what I needed from the store. If I was stuck, I'd wander the aisles until something sparked inspiration. Then I would plan, always plan.

Client laying shiny stepping stones for fairies alongside the railroad garden.
Courtesy of Kathryn Rogers.

But now pieces of nature I'd previously overlooked pique my curiosity, creativity, and even spontaneity. I listen to the spirit of each material because it knows better than I do where it belongs.

Seashells become lakes with walnut casings as the boats assail. Pebbles make cobblestone pathways that lead to spiral staircases of padauk shavings left over from woodshop. However, it's at the top of the staircase and in the gardens surrounding the walkways that the real magic occurs.

It doesn't matter that my canvas is a plastic, orange frisbee because petals from dried flowers are my watercolors while dried berries and corn kernels are my oil pastels. Curlicue twigs become lampposts with iridescent shells as the sources of illumination.

Who knows what I'll stumble upon during my next meander through the garden, perhaps on my way to class? My eyes now know to notice the tiniest bits of sparkle.

I quickly become immersed in the details, intricacies, and elegance that develop out of the intertwining of each little forgotten bit of nature. They transform quickly into a fairy house with all the requisite resplendence.

Seeing my work in progress, I feel again like I have glitter in my hair and am dancing with the fairies of my childhood imagination. I'm rediscovering simple beauty and uncovering misplaced whimsy when I visit my fairy land.

-- *Jenny M.*

AWE LEADS TO TRUST

Fairy gardening and home-building are very much in keeping with the Skyland Trail philosophy that allows clients to choose and identify small goals in their journey to recovery, beginning with admission. Maria describes the process of building her first fairy home with the sunflower seed-head roof and an arched entryway decorated with hydrangea petals as the first opportunity to "see the color of creativity" in her recovery from depression. "There are so many layers — first there is the house and rooftop, then the window box [made with a hickory hull], and now the landscape with paths, trees and a mailbox."

Jenny making her fairy home with kernels of Indian corn, crepe myrtle seed pods, and wood slips from the wood shop.

Angela found unexpected materials coming together in her fairy home, including red bud seed pods, corn kernels, and agapanthus. *Courtesy of Sarah Lasswell.*

Layering is a description many clients use in building fairy homes and gardens. Observing and surveying the clients for five years, I have identified the creative process as follows: at first an appreciation of nature when choosing materials, then a period of curiosity and ingenuity, and finally a connection — a purposeful re-creation of the materials. This sequence parallels the "What Skills" learned in DBT with the goal of increasing the ability to relate to positive emotions through three steps: observe, describe, and participate. Through fairy gardening and home-building activities, clients are actively continuing nature's creation and inviting imaginative, non-judgmental guests — the fairies. It is a positive experience overall, a connection that brings forth tools for recovery.

Although the life of Jessica's fairy treehouse was short, she writes, "It taught me about the ephemeral nature of even the prettiest things we create. There was a rainstorm and it actually collapsed a couple of days after we built it. It went down quickly so we didn't have much time to enjoy it; but in a way that made the time in which we did admire it more special." Jessica relates the experience of her fairy home re-building to her recovery journey: "I had two [relapses] very close to one another so that as soon as I healed from one, I had another. Similarly, my fairy home collapsed just as we refurbished it. Having both experiences taught me patience with the process of healing, and to persevere even through setbacks, because they may be inevitable, but you will heal."

Sweetgum balls border paths in the railroad garden.
Courtesy of Kathryn Rogers.

Vadi's surf board made with twisted wisteria seed pod and pine bark.
Courtesy of Kathryn Rogers.

Nature can be genuinely empathetic; it relapses every year and then springs forward, full of hope. Like Jessica, many clients at Skyland Trail seek solace in the metaphors found in fairy gardening and home-building. The activity truthfully illustrates the recovery journey while keeping a fresh coat of hope alive. Clients learn to be ready for the unexpected and to trust in the unknown. Angela writes about her experience of building a fairy home, "I found some things didn't work as expected. This gave me an opportunity to try different materials and techniques." Explained Tony, "The 'recovery road' leads to places and experiences that you can't anticipate."

"Enjoy the experience," Vadi adds, as he launches his fairy surfboard onto "the ocean's chaotic waves."

It is not an easy, predictable ride, this journey of recovery from mental illness. Yet, in tandem with fairy gardening and home-building, the experience through recovery has momentum generated by hope — and a chance to embrace awe in the moment amidst the magic offered up by fairies.

1. Visit our website: www.SkylandTrail.org

2. 70% of clients admitted in 2012 were between the ages of 18 and 35. Source: 2012 Annual Report

3. Bipolar illness constitutes 45% of the diagnosis at admission, followed by Major Depression, 36%.

4. For more information on the DBT Recovery Community at Skyland Trail, visit: www.SkylandTrail.org/DBT.aspx.

THE FAIRY DEW DROP

Down by the spring one morning
Where the shadows still lay deep,
I found in the heart of a flower
A tiny fairy asleep.

Her flower couch was perfumed,
Leaf curtains drawn with care,
And there she sweetly slumbered,
With a jewel in her hair.

But a sunbeam entered softly
And touched her as she lay,
Whispering that 'twas morning
And fairies must away.

All colors of the rainbow
Were in her robe so bright
As she danced away with the sunbeam
And vanished from my sight.

'Twas while I watched them dancing,
The sunshine told me true,
That my sparkling little fairy
Was lovely Drop O'Dew.

~ Laura Ingalls Wilder, February 1915

A * P * P * E * N * D * I * X

The Designers

ALISON BARRY AND BRIAN MAIN ——————————— Elventree
www.elventree.co.uk

We have been creating fairy dwellings for six years now. One day we took a walk along the riverbank and found a beautifully shaped piece of driftwood. We came up with the idea of using the wood in its natural form to create a fairy house, and Elventree was born! Our initial inspiration for the houses came from a love of wood, nature, and the area in which we live. It seemed natural to us to create a fairy house as we both love nature spirits and fairies. We believe that every tree has its own fairy spirit to protect and nurture the wood and the ground in which it stands.

CAROL BETSINGER——————————— FaeryGrrlGardens
www.etsy.com/shop/FaeryGrrlGardens

I grew up as a child of nature playing in the forests near my Illinois home. Fallen trees became my secret world, and the beauty of the woodland nourished my imagination.

My life was blessed with two beautiful daughters and five grandchildren. My oldest daughter died at the age of thirty in 2007 from complications of cystic fibrosis. She had a great passion for fairies. A fairy house that she purchased at a Minnesota Renaissance Festival was one of her prized treasures and the first fairy house that I had ever seen. After her death, it seemed natural to combine my forever love of her with my innate love of nature to create my own unique fairy houses.

Fairy folklore has given me an understanding of the ways of the fairies, and I work to incorporate their whimsical spirit into each house I build. To date, I have constructed twenty-five detailed fairy houses, each one created from garden and expired woodland materials.

TORI CARPENTER——————— Torisaur: Fine Goods for Rare Beings
www.torisaur.com

I design and build sculptures, fairy houses, and furnishings for all variety of rare beings. Creations are lovingly hand-crafted in my woodland studio using forest bits and fairy dust (which was acquired some time ago).

JOHN C. CRAWFORD——————————— Fairy Woodland
www.fairywoodland.com

Each fairy house I build begins with the discovery of a twig whose marvelous shape or character grabs my imagination. The rest of the creation process is a constant interaction between the vision I see in the twigs and the practical considerations of durability and other technical problems in realizing the house. This puzzle spurred me to create a sculptural process of working in a bed of sand, allowing me to follow the contours of the twigs when forming the walls.

The craft operations of making a fairy house are the simplest part of it; what's most important to me is keeping alive the whole life history of the twigs and stones from which it is constructed. I suspect that my mindset comes from my life-long work as a puppeteer, learning to animate everything I touched. It's the same with the fairy houses — I'm not just trying to make a model, I'm creating a living creature. It's not a birdhouse; it's a fairy house, and it's intended for the habitation of fairies. I seek to render a house that is as real as the fairies that I meet: dusty, well used, eroded by the winds of time.

The titles of my pieces come from the stories they tell. When I finish a house, my wife and creative partner, Bridget Wolfe, sits with it and listens for the story and then writes it down. Each piece comes with a journal, which contains the story she finds and lots of blank pages for the new "keeper" of the house to continue the tale and pass it on to new generations. Our intention is to create a mystical "gateway" to allow the mortal imagination and denizens of the fairy realm to find each other again.

EMILY CROOKER——————————————— Enchanted Gourds
www.enchantedgourds.com

Enchanted Gourds was born in 2006 when my nieces became quite taken with the fairies. In imagining what kind of houses they might like, the thought of inviting the fairies inside our houses kept coming up. One has to wonder if they were whispering in our ears at night. Imagine the mischief they could make if given a cozy spot within the house! Knowing that our cats love little fluttering wings, hanging gourds seemed the wise choice. Gourds have long been used as vessels and musical instruments as they are a rather versatile and sturdy canvas. Gourd art and fairy culture both have incredible histories, spanning many cultures and centuries. As no two fairies are alike, so are no two gourds, or gourd fairy houses for that matter, which makes crafting them an adventure. Each house is unique and designed to a theme using mostly natural or vintage materials. Amazing things can be made from others' "junk," and fairies appreciate a little crafty recycling.

SANDY DARLING——————————————— Woodland Kreatures
www.woodlandkreatures.com

I create one-of-a-kind fantasy art dolls and creatures. I am a self-taught artist in polymer clay and other mixed media. I have always had a love and fascination for the strange and unusual, the cute and the ugly. I was and am a huge fan of Jim Henson and all of his wonderful creations. As a child, I would play by myself for hours in my imaginary world with my imaginary characters. My love for these whimsical beings has never changed, neither has my ever-growing imagination. I always had the desire to create these characters that existed only in my mind, but didn't know how to make that happen — and then I was introduced to polymer clay and made my first miniature creation. I haven't put the clay down since! To be able to take a lump of clay and bits of wire and fabric and turn it into a fantasy art doll has been one of my life's most rewarding experiences and with every fairy I make, I write a short story to go along with him or her.

ELAINE ENGLAND——————————— New England Nurseries
www.newenglandnurseries.com

When asked if I would lead a fairy garden workshop, I jumped at the chance. There is a plethora of information available on fairies if you know where to look. My husband and I are the proud grandparents of nine grandchildren. I found them to be an enthusiastic source of inspiration. One granddaughter told me to simply "think like a fairy and make the garden a place they would want to be."

MARE FAULDS——————————— Woodland Fairy Village
www.woodlandfairyvillage.com

I have been creating my fairy houses for a few years, and I love every moment. My collection is called the Woodland Fairy Village, and each house tells a story uniquely its own. It is my hope that each of the stories is read with magical eyes and wonderment. Designing fairy houses has allowed me the pleasure of escaping into a creative fantasy world, a magical woodland realm where forest fairies and creatures exist. Miniatures have always fascinated me, especially miniature creatures who roam these fantasy worlds. The woodland fairies that I imagine inhabiting my fairy houses make their homes not only from their forest surroundings, but also from items collected from the human realm. I envision these fairies as enchanting, whimsical, brilliant, and practical.

GINGER FULLER——————————— Upside Down Daisy
www.etsy.com/shop/BonnieBlu12

A wife and mother, I live in a small town in southern Indiana. I am from a family full of various types of artists. I am a folk artist, which, simply put, means I have no formal training. However, I have loved doing anything art related for as long as I can remember and I work with many mediums, but I must admit this fairy stuff is so much fun to make — one is only limited by their imagination.

LINDA HAAS——————————— Tree Star Hollow
www.treestarhollow.com

As an artist and landscape designer, I have found my niche in fairy gardening. I started to make miniature gardens as a child, creating fairy homesteads using things I gathered in the woods. To this day, I am happiest in the forest. Fairy gardening has become a family tradition with my daughters and granddaughters. In 2012, I opened

Tree Star Hollow, a fairy garden and boutique, where I hold workshops each month.

ROB HEARD——————————— The Pavilion
www.robheard.co.uk/bough_house.html

I live with my family in a timber-framed house that I built myself on the grounds of the fourteenth-century family manor house on the edge of Exmoor. Working from my workshop in the estate gardens, I create my Bough House sculptures, inspired by the rolling countryside surrounding my home.

My initial inspiration begins with the wood itself, sourced locally in a sustainable way. The natural twists and curves of the timber inspire each design, which encompasses turrets, aerial walkways, staircases, bridges, and a massive array of intricately designed elements. Because each starting point is different, each house is unique, and I find myself guided by the wood as the story of each house unfolds.

My art is to be touched, to be played with. My girls love to play with their Bough House — they call it their Fairy House — and they also help to test each new house as it appears. The quality of the workmanship on the first house has stood the test of time and playtime. Yet I feel the Bough Houses are more than a physical thing — they enchant people. You can spend hours wandering the walkways and turrets and paths in your own mind. These are truly inspirational pieces of art. My only limit is the height of my workshop ceiling and maybe that's a blessing!

LYNSEY HIGGINSON——————————— Awen Alive
www.awenalive.co.uk

I love working in clay as it is a natural product and comes from the earth. In 2008, my husband and I started Awen Alive, a pagan- and fairy-inspired pottery that we sell at fairs and, through our website, all over the world. I have had connections with the fairy folk all of my life, and the woods and forests are where I feel closest to them. I want my fairy houses to look like something you would stumble upon while on a walk through a magical forest. All my fairy houses are based on a woodland theme and are tree stumps that have been occupied by the fairy folk! I make a range of homes from starter homes for first-time fairy buyers up to woodland mansions for the more discerning fairy.

TATIANA KATARA _____ The FAERIE Factory™
www.fairyfactory.com

As an eco-artist, transforming trash into treasure is one of my main goals. My work is made almost entirely of recycled and natural materials that would otherwise return to nature or end up in landfills. Once I started making fairy furniture, I couldn't stop. As a single mother of two, I couldn't afford to spend money on traditional art materials, but did have access to nature, scraps of old clothes, and pieces of sheetrock and plaster from working on my own house. These provided an ample start to my fairy house creations. As my work began to sell in galleries, my fairy workshops took off, often selling out. Over a decade, I released thousands of inspired fairy house-builders into the movement, who have, in turn, helped to create a world of lush Internet photos. My background in film as a scenic and props artist set me up perfectly to make fairy art. Since 2000, I have created an inventory of mini pirate ships, Ferris wheels, a mad scientists' castle, lighthouses, bridges, fairy pirate shipyards, buggies, carts, hot air balloons, a fairy zoo, steam punk fairy structures, a fairy capitol building, a fairy Taj Mahal, restaurants, shops, and even a fairy amusement park.

DERRIEN KILSBY & TERRY SEVERINSKI _____ Homes for Gnomes
homesforgnomes.weebly.com

Homes for Gnomes are whimsical garden cottages made from recycled cedar and hardware. Each one of our homes is unique, having been lovingly designed and crafted with great attention to detail. They vary in size, from 11" to 24" tall. Beside a garden pond, along a woodland trail, or tucked away in a small perennial garden, our homes are sure to delight any passerby, young and old alike.

SHERYL LOZIER _____ Summers Past Farms
www.summerspastfarms.com

Children love to look at and smell the flowers in my gardens at Summers Past Farms in Southern California. Our nursery is full of various colorful blossoms every season, so every season children (and their parents) wander through, just enjoying the flowers. Because I enjoy sharing my love of flowers and gardening with everyone, I started creating container gardens with themes in 2000. My first creation was in a wooden wine crate, and I planted it with small pebble paths and thyme, santolina, and violas trimmed as hedges. Small benches and tiny pots made my garden look like a formal French garden at Villandry. I began collecting small chairs, benches, tables, arbors, and, of course, fairies to sell in my store. I offered classes, and everyone wanted to create a small container garden with fairies. A

few years later, we hosted our first fairy festival and now we hold it annually, on the first Saturday in June. Children come dressed in colorful dresses, with fairy wings, halos with ribbons, and flowers in their hair. They bring fairy gardens they've made at home, which are judged by where a fairy would most want to live.

PAULA MALTA _____ Two Crazy Hearts
tchearts@socal.rr.com
www.etsy.com/shop/TwoCrazyHearts

Crafting, creating, nature, people, good food, and animals were the staples in my family and young life. My love of collecting, gardening, and old things came from my creative crafty mom. This was a jump-start to more of my passions and loves.

At the age of five, I discovered, and was inspired by, claymation films, so I made my own little mini foods with my beloved playdough. In the second grade, I read *The Littles* by John Peterson and that reinforced my affinity with the tiny world, as there were so many possibilities. I see the world and my surroundings at different angles and the mediums/materials I use vary — vastly. I picture something in my head — many things inspire me — and there it is. Today, I combine my love of design (a biggie), decorating, arranging, nature, and an eye for vintage with creating vignettes of all kinds: crafting miniatures, floral arrangements, mosaics, and whatever else my brain comes up with.

DANI MENDENHALL _____ Dragonfly Hollow at Dragonfly Shops & Gardens
www.dragonflyshopsandgardens.com

I have been playing in the garden my entire life, but it's just been in the past few years that I've been focusing on creating fairy gardens. In fact, falling in love with everything about the miniature/fairy garden world and creating gardens of all sizes with miniature plants and decorations led me to open my business, Dragonfly Hollow, where I teach people how to do what I love.

I love to create gardens with various scenes or themes around special occasions, holidays, activities, etc. I particularly love to create various scenes in which the plants play to the container and to the miniature items. The people who come to my fairy garden classes or purchase one of my miniature gardens notice that every item in the garden is placed deliberately — even the small bits of gravel and rocks are placed just right. If you look at my gardens, you will see fun items peeking out. It might take a few glances to notice all of the details. I gratefully acknowledge the assistance of Jennifer Anastasi in preparing my entry.

ARTHUR MILLICAN JR.
Sleepy Hollow Enterprises LLC
www.whimsicalfairygarden.com

Having the opportunity to work for and having been a part of designing magical experiences with the Walt Disney Company, I was given the skills and the abilities to bring these magical worlds to life. A lot of my inspiration comes from nature itself. What would you build to live in if you were the size of a Fairy? Would you want to live under a pile sticks? Or would you rather live in a hole like a Troll? Maybe, you would try and find discarded items, like old teapots or food cans, to give you that homey start. If you were a Leprechaun and a skilled cobbler, would you not use your skills to build yourself an elegant home? To look at one of these found items and see the "what if" can be a great start to your whimsical creation. Many of the Magical Fairy houses I have built are out of found items from flea markets, discarded items, and bits and bobs found in the woods. Acorns can make great lamps and whimsical details. Bottle caps become umbrellas, widows, or mirrors. I use a variety of painting techniques from airbrushing to using dry-brush blending to obtain that camouflage or Old World look.

JAY O'ROURKE
New England Nurseries
www.newenglandnurseries.com

The world of fairy gardening opened up to me on an annual trip with my daughter to the New England Flower Show. One of the vendors had some adorable miniature furniture that we just had to have. I added a miniature cottage and trough to the collection later. Ever since, planting the fairy garden has been one of my favorite spring activities. Now, many springs later, I am exhibiting in the Boston Flower Show with New England Nurseries, where I have worked for over twenty years.

BETH POMROY
BEEZ, INC.
www.beezinc.com

Do I believe in fairies? No...but I do believe in imagination and something like the "divine." I recently lost my mother and needed a positive outlet, a way to go on through grief. I don't know really what sparked the fairy room building, I just started. Can Mom see these? Wouldn't she love them? Wouldn't she be proud! That's what I mean by divine. Those thoughts are comforting. It gives me so much pleasure to watch people of all ages smile and point while looking at them, peering from all angles. In return, I do a lot of smiling, which is great therapy!

I started using the usual materials I saw other people use, natural things: birch bark, seeds, sticks, and shells. This collecting got me outside. Walks are useful for collecting, but also for connecting to nature and the island I live on, which also helps my mind. Soon, I found what really turned me on was the making of tiny little things to go in the houses: furniture, accessories, tools. Now I use all sorts of materials — natural, found, and recycled. I look at junk and see a sink or a wheelbarrow part. My handmade paper is good for books and toilet paper rolls. What kind of shell looks like a candle flame? A piece of sea glass could be a bar of soap. Everything is new to me, I see the world differently.

BETH POWELL
FAERIE Odd Mother
bjpowell@charter.net

I've been an avid artist from a very young age. I think making these fairy houses was a natural progression of my art. As a child, I was very influenced by the living arrangements on *The Swiss Family Robinson* (Johann Wyss), *The Borrowers* (Mary Norton), and *The Root Children* (Sibylle Von Olfers). I spent hours making homes, rooms, and treehouses out of cardboard, jewelry boxes, paper towel rolls, matchboxes, and anything else I could find. I made all the furniture too, including sewing and embroidering miniature bedspreads, curtains, canopies, etc.

Fast-forward. I now have children of my own. When they were younger, we would go outside and practice "random acts of art" in the woods. Fairy houses were our favorite. My houses became more sophisticated and a passion was renewed, only this time I used natural materials to build into. I discovered my talent for seeing hidden potential for almost every little natural thing I come in contact with. Materials talk to me...I'm a twig whisperer. I cannot go anywhere without an eye to the ground. I am always on the hunt for materials — the old standbys and the super unique — to incorporate into my next piece. I build places I would like to live in with a rich variety of earthy colors and textures, visually pleasing with luxurious creature comforts and lots of places for a fairy to hang out. Nothing is in scale, of course, to accommodate fairies of all shapes and sizes. I think of most of my houses as fairy communes, so please, come discover my world!

DAVID RAU
Florence Griswold Museum
www.flogris.org

I am the Director of Education & Outreach at the Florence Griswold Museum in Old Lyme and, most recently, the coordinator of the Museum's outdoor October events: Wee Faerie Village (2009), Scarecrows at the Museum (2010), Of Feathers and Faerie Tales: Enchanted Birdhouses (2011), Wee Faerie Village in the Land of Picture Making (2012), and Wee Faerie Village in the Land of Oz (2013). I also participate in the events as an artist, honing my skills by building fairy houses, sculpting scarecrows, and decorating birdhouses.

MIKE & DEBBIE SCHRAMER —————————— Enchanted Treehouse
www.enchantedtreehousemovie.com

Nature is a retreat for us. We love to gather the beautiful materials we use for our fairy houses from our beautiful gardens and from walks along the beach and through the forest. The lovely flowers (our favorite in nature), the sweet smelling herbs in our gardens, and the wild plants in the neighboring fields are all healing for us. It is as if the world of nature speaks a language that we somehow understand. Our fairy houses are an expression of our longing for the lovely gardens of our dreams, that place that we draw to within ourselves to feel loved and happy. Working on our fairy houses together is a wondrous and amazing adventure; we often feel like curious children who have suddenly discovered a new and amazing world.

LIBBA SHORTRIDGE ——————————————— Skyland Trail
www.skylandtrail.org

I am a registered, full-time horticultural therapist at Skyland Trail in Atlanta, Georgia, where I been able to combine my awe of nature and human nature since 2007. I am very grateful for the supportive staff at Skyland Trail in my exploration of fairy gardening and home-building as therapy. I would like to recognize the many volunteers, interns, and community leaders — my "fairy muses" — without whom this project would not have come to fruition: Carole Weil, Shea Pool, Amy Mitchell, Rachel Olson, Barb Bohannon, Ruby Bock, Virginia Pyron, Sarah Lasswell, Margaret Zona, Wendy Battaglia, Amy Blumenfeld, Dorothy Pritchett, Alison Turner, Seran Megerian, Kathryn Rogers, and Clara St. Urbain.

SIMON SINKINSON —————————— Tiny Doors for Tiny Things
www.tinydoors.com

Deep in the forest lie many tiny doors, the homes of the quietest, smallest, shyest creatures. As you amble through the woods, keep your eyes peeled for signs of tiny life — a little wooden wheelbarrow filled with acorns or a tiny napkin left after a fairy tea. I have come across signs of tiny life in most woods that I have gotten to know — wild woods offer a safe haven for most small creatures.
I have been fitting tiny doors to all manner of crevices for thirty-five years. When I was a boy, my bed collapsed

— it lost a leg and my father wouldn't buy me another bed — so a log was slid under that corner. Being a fan of *Pogles' Wood*, a 1960s BBC television show for children about simple tiny creatures that live in a tree, I, of course, had to fit a little door in my log! I loved sleeping in my bed above this little home. It made me feel as if I was high on the top of a tree canopy. I have been making my little homes (doors) ever since.

SALLY J. SMITH ———————————————— Greenspirit Arts
www.greenspiritarts.com

I work year-round primarily in the Boquet river basin in the northeast corner of the Adirondacks. I create ephemeral sculptures from found and collected natural materials. Most of the works are created on site, though some of the more elaborate pieces are created in my studio and then moved to the location for which they were designed.
How do I create the works? Basically, I just pay attention: To the movement of the sun, moon, and stars. To the growing cycles of the plants. To changes in wind and temperature. To patterns and forms inherent in the landscape. To building materials that are abundantly at hand wherever I look.
I bring a few small hand tools. In the summer, I might have small rose pruners for sharp snipping or a needle and cotton thread to stitch leaves together, or thorns to do the same. In the winter, I bring an ice axe or small handsaws to harvest icicles from along the lakes and rivers.
All these ideas, plus generous dollops of whimsy and fantasy, are woven into each unique piece to reflect a natural sense of "home." When the sculpture is complete, I apply my last tool: a digital SLR camera. My image attempts to convey the moment of magic when landscape, material, and artist were fused into an experience of Oneness. Whenever possible, the sculptures are left to return to the earth, which gave them birth, as an offering of gratitude.

JENNIE STOCKSLAGER —— Stockslager's Greenhouse & Garden Center
www.stockslagers.com

Fairy gardening began for me in September 2011. Before that date, I was unaware of the phenomena, but in less than a month, my husband and his family's garden center began introducing customers to this new aspect of the greenhouse industry that creates joy for all who embrace it.
I appreciate the magic of fairy gardening that speaks to our "inner child," asking our imagination to "come out and play." Who amongst us, as a child, did not believe in fairies? Or at least, in the depths of the heart, did not believe in the possibility of fairies? I remember watching the black-and-white movie version of *Peter Pan* in my grandparents'

living room, circa 1950s. Poor Tinkerbell was in the glass jar, slowing dying after drinking the poison Captain Hook intended for Peter. As Tink's light was fading, Peter looked directly at the television audience and implored us to save Tinkerbell! All we had to do was say we believed in fairies! I'm not ashamed to say that I fervently vowed my belief and consequently basked in relief as I watched Tinkerbell's life force glow stronger and stronger!

Tinkerbell didn't die that day, but somewhere through the years, the part of me that believed in magic forgot the thrill of my imagination transporting me to worlds unknown, worlds where anything is possible, and then right before me was fairy gardening, combining both nature and the opportunity to feel childlike. I experienced a tug in my heart and the sense of joy that only magic can create.

MARGOT VAN DE WIEL —————————————— Filz-Art
www.etsy com/shop/FilzArts

I started creating fairy houses about eight years ago. While experimenting with felt, I created my first fairy house. Children visiting my studio were so enthusiastic about it that they inspired me to create more fairy houses. What I like most about fairy houses is that you can create such fairy-tale atmospheres, with colors and forms, that permit humans to enter another world. This escape into the world of imagination can be very healthy.

BETH WITSIK —————————————— Whimsical Properties, LLC
www.whimsicalproperties.blogspot.com

On a bright summer morning, when I was in the backyard at our lake house with my two young children, I noticed a partially hollow log. As I bent down to peer inside, I offhandedly asked, "Do you think fairies live in here?" Four little eyes grew huge. In that moment, surrounded by the sweet fragrance of grass and earth, magic sprouted and so did Whimsical Properties. We watched that log, and soon the fairies revealed themselves to us by leaving little signs of their presence. In turn, we left them useful fairy-size things — a milk pod to use as a chair, a feather as a fan, a silver gum wrapper to serve as a mirror. Collecting these items inspired me to create a couple of fairy houses as gifts and, before I knew it, I had a huge inventory of fairy real estate!

Every Whimsical Property is named and includes a descriptive MLS listing along with photographs. Plus, it's in move-in condition, fully furnished and decorated — usually with handcrafted elements.

ROXIE J. ZWICKER —————————————— Spirited Woodland
www.spiritedwoodland.etsy.com

I've been creating art since I can remember and I am always collecting little things and filling drawers with all my finds. When I am sitting down working on a project, it's very much like a meditation for me. The entire outside world escapes, and I am in my own little magical space, envisioning some fantastic place of wondrous little beings. When I'm working with pinecones or acorns, I feel that they each have a story to tell. Putting my finds together they form a delightful, one-of-a-kind place I see in my mind. I could tell you exactly where I found each piece of wood, shell, or acorn. My houses have pieces of many places: milkweed fluff from a hillside in Vermont, tree lichen from Cape Cod, or driftwood from the coast of Maine. Some decorations are little odd pieces from thrift and antique shops. All of the wood in my fairy houses is from fallen branches or found on the ground…I never harm living trees. My hope is that upon each closer look the viewer has to look twice because they see something they haven't noticed before. Whether it is a tiny gemstone or a fluttering butterfly, there is so much to see if we just stop to take a closer look.

Acknowledgments

Each new book is a novel experience, an adventure, and a challenge. There is a reason why we selected these artists for this book. Their work is exciting, whimsical, and fascinating. They use different materials in different ways and create magical places. They challenge us to use our imaginations and to think about a world we seldom see... the world of the fairies. We also know that the Schiffer design department will make their images stand out!

David D. J. Rau drew on his own experience in writing the Introduction. We chuckled out loud upon reading it. We also want to thank Cary Hull, who began this book with Ashley.

Front Cover Credit: Sally J. Smith

Back Cover: Linda Haas, Tatiana Katara, Sheryl Lozier (Whitbeck Photography), Simon Sinkinson, Sally J. Smith, Beth Witsik

About the Authors

Barbara Purchia, a stained glass artist, has wanted to write a book for a long time. She has been well known for her technical articles, papers, and presentations on software process improvements. She has edited Ashley Rooney's "100 Artists" series books, as well as many other books, and was delighted at the opportunity to co-author this book with Ashley.

Ashley Rooney has established a solid reputation for her architectural, art, and design books, as well as her historical works. She has written many art books, including *100 New England Artists* (2010), *100 Mid-Atlantic Artists* (2011), *100 Midwestern Artists* (2012), *100 Southern Artists* (2012), *Bespoke Furniture from 103 Artisans* (2012), *100 Northwestern Artists* (2013), *Green Art: Trees, Leaves, and Bark* (2013), *Contemporary Art of the Southwest* (2014), and *Artists Homes and Studios* (2014). In this work, she draws upon her gardening expertise.

Artists' Index